D0369975

LETTING GO WITH LOVE

Letting Go with Love

Help for Those Who Love an Alcoholic/Addict, Whether Practicing or Recovering

Julia H.

Introduction by Randy Davis, Ph.D.

JEREMY P. TARCHER, INC.
Los Angeles
Distributed by St. Martin's Press
New York

DEDICATION

I discovered that writing a book is like living with a chemical dependent. It's lonely, isolating, frustrating, maddening, and obsessive. Nevertheless, I am forever grateful that I was given the opportunity to experience both in one lifetime.

Lest you think that "Letting Go with Love" means *leaving* the chemical dependent, let me assure you, having stayed with one for thirty years, that it does not.

Lest you think that "Letting Go with Love" means *staying* with the chemical dependent, who knows what tomorrow will bring?

I dedicate this book to my husband, without whom there would not have been a book.

Library of Congress Cataloging in Publication Data

H., Julia.
   Letting go with love.

   Bibliography
   1. Alcoholics—United States—Family relationships.
   2. Alcoholics—Rehabilitation—United States.
   3. Alcoholism—Treatment—United States. I. Title.
HV5132.H2   1987   362.2'92   87-9944
ISBN 0-87477-425-X

Jeremy P. Tarcher, Inc.
9110 Sunset Blvd.
Los Angeles, CA 90069

Design by Robert Tinnon

Manufactured in the United States of America
10   9   8   7   6   5   4   3   2   1

First Edition

Contents

Acknowledgments

I want to thank Big Al, Bill W., Dr. Bob, Eve, Liz, Elle, Charlotte, Darlene, J.P., other friends, and my family, for giving me a lift along the way.

A Note

This book is based on my experience in Al-Anon, a fellowship of nonprofessional, self-supporting, self-help groups for the relatives and friends of alcoholics. Al-Anon members share their knowledge and experience with one another but do not offer advice or counseling.

I do not speak for Al-Anon, and Al-Anon neither affiliates nor endorses any cause, project, or individual.

To protect the anonymity of those in the program, I use no real people and no real names in this book, including my own.

Introduction

Letting Go with Love is part of a revolution that has been going on in recent years, in large part unnoticed by society, a revolution in self-care, a revolution of people who, individually and in groups, are taking the securing of their mental health into their own hands. Julia H.'s experience is a testimony to the possibilities, the drama, and the excitement that this self-caring can bring about.

Everybody knows by now that we live in a society with serious alcoholism and drug addiction problems, a society in which for every substance abuser there are dozens of others whose lives are deeply affected. Parents worry about children, children worry about parents, husbands worry about wives, wives worry about husbands, and friends worry about each other.

For many years, professional psychologists were barely aware of this vast pool of suffering. We concentrated on making the alcoholic/addict better, and thought that when we were able to do that their families and friends—those we now call *co-dependents*—would by and large begin to feel better, too.

In the last few years, many of us have come to realize that we had neglected to recognize the anguish, confusion, and worry of the co-dependents. We had excluded these loved ones from the health-care delivery system.

Today we realize that co-dependents need as much help as alcoholics/addicts. Fortunately, this realization had already come to a great many who were suffering from "co-dependency" and who had banded together in their own recovery groups, in programs such as Julia H. insightfully describes.

Participating in these groups has been vital in comprehensive treatment programs for many co-dependents. Identifying with others in their peer group has provided the necessary link between their pain and its resolution.

As a psychologist, my practice is focused on individual and family therapy. However, I also strongly recommend the twelve-step process that is the basis of this book. Such twelve-step, self-help, anonymous groups—with their breadth of shared experience, their ability to help us see ourselves in others' eyes and others' lives, and with their tremendous support, humor and warmth—can provide co-dependents with newfound feelings of safety and security so important to their mental health.

As the co-dependents expose their experiences, they begin to feel a sense of power and strength that has often been buried. These groups also give co-dependents the opportunity to listen to the experiences of others, which adds to their willingness to bring about changes in their relationship with the alcoholic/addict.

These changes often create new levels of understanding as well as new, more adaptive behaviors. After a co-dependent participated in a self-help program, I have often been amazed to see the growth in a relationship so dysfunctional that one might have lost hope that it could ever be healed.

Julia is not a psychological professional, so you may ask, "What does *she* know? She's just like me." And that's the point.

What Julia knows—what tens of thousands of Julias and Johns know—is the *experience* of co-dependency as a way of life. Julia knows it from the inside, as she knows the processes of self-discovery, self-revelation, and ultimately, self-healing. Even with my professional background and daily practice in these areas, *Letting Go with Love* has deepened my awareness of these processes.

Realistic above all, *Letting Go with Love* provides hope for change without underestimating the difficulties of growth. It provides tools for change while recognizing how hard it can be to use them. It offers guidance for change while understanding that each person must ultimately make his own way. And it offers companionship for change with the knowledge that support from others with similar problems is perhaps the surest way to success.

Of course, the symptoms of co-dependency vary from person to person and not all problems can be fully resolved at group meetings. If you are depressed and anxious—with symptoms such as sleep disturbance, appetite changes, loss of energy, or irritability—it is important that you get a thorough physical examination by your personal physician. Additionally, you might also want to consider setting up an appointment with a professional therapist: a psychiatrist, psychologist, social worker, or marriage and family counselor. To obtain a referral, ask your physician or contact the local chapter of the American Psychological Association. The therapist you choose should be experienced in dealing with issues surrounding alcoholism and addiction.

Another caution. Once you take action to help yourself, changes in your attitudes and behavior may be uncomfortable for the alcoholic/addict in your life. He is just as used to your old behavior patterns as you are to his. His discomfort is natural, and it may be what is necessary for him to seek help, just as yours was.

You do not have to be a co-dependent to benefit from the tools presented here. When my wife read *Letting Go with Love* in manuscript, she said that it raised issues relevant to all relationships, including our own. She was right.

The courage to recover is in each of us. Your decision to read this book may be your first exposure to your own courage. Allow Julia H. to provide through her experiences the support that will help you on your own journey.

Randy Davis, Ph.D.

Welcome Aboard

If you love an alcoholic/addict, whether practicing or recovering, you may be wondering how it is possible to be filled with so much rage, frustration, and fear toward the very same person you love so deeply. It is this contradiction that causes the confusion, the turmoil, and the endless stream of questions—questions you may be too afraid or too ashamed to ask. If that's the case, I have some questions for you.

QUESTIONS FOR THE READER

Are you filled with resentment toward an alcoholic/addict in your life?

Are you loaded with guilt, yet don't know why?

Do you spend time counting his drinks, watering his drinks, pouring his booze down the drain, matching him drink for drink?

Do you find yourself lying for her, making excuses for her, coaxing, bribing, yelling at her to stop?

Do you believe you can cure a user, control how much a user uses, or make a user stop using?

Do you worry constantly about somebody's addiction?

Have you lost the trust you once had for your daughter since she's become an addict?

Do you feel that you've failed your son, a substance abuser?

Do you believe you're the cause of your mother's addiction?

Are you experiencing a lot of anxiety?

Do you feel like a doormat?

Do you feel isolated or trapped with your feelings?

Do you blame the addict for your misery?

Is your anger, once saved for the alcoholic, beginning to spread?

Do you get colds or viruses more often?

Are you more and more afraid to go out in public with the abuser?

Do you secretly wish that the addict would be punished for what he has done to you?

Do you dislike or distrust your daughter's new friends in her recovery program?

Do you feel that you are being neglected by your husband now that he has found a recovery program?

Do you feel disappointed that your son's recovery isn't the answer to all your problems?

Did you like the alcoholic better before he found a recovery program?

If you answered yes to any of the preceding questions, you're not alone. You may feel that you are, but you're not. There are many, many others in the same boat.

In the United States there are an estimated 20 million practicing alcoholics/addicts. There are over 2 million more in recovery programs.

There are husbands and wives, mothers and fathers, sons and daughters, brothers and sisters, lovers and friends whose lives are being seriously affected by the alcoholics/addicts they love. A conservative figure is five family members or friends for every alcoholic/addict, practicing or recovering.

Multiply 22 million by five, and you'll see how filled to capacity the boat really is. At least 110 million passengers share similar experiences, but they don't know they do, because they don't share their experiences with anyone. They're afraid to, or they're ashamed to. That's why they think they're alone. They're not. If they were to confide in one another, here are some of the deep, dark secrets they'd tell:

"Holidays are the worst. Dad gets drunk and Mom yells at him. I always think it'll be different, but it never is."

"We have to hide our wallets in our own house! Our daughter is desperate for money to buy more drugs. We try to reason with her, but she won't listen."

"My husband makes me call his office and tell them he has a bad case of flu. Flu, my ass! He has a bad case of booze."

"Our sex life is the pits. He doesn't want me when he's sober, and I don't want him when he's drunk."

"I had to bail my son out again."

"My friends tell me she's an alcoholic, but I don't believe it. All she has to do is cut down like I did."

"I don't think my daughter would have a drug problem if she'd choose other friends. They talk her into it every time."

"I thought when my husband joined A.A. that everything would be wonderful again. He's definitely getting better, but I'm still miserable."

"I went with my daughter to a Narcotics Anonymous meeting. When she said, 'My name is Jenny and I'm an addict,' I felt a profound sense of failure."

"How can my son do this to me? I've always been a good father."

If any of these passengers' secrets is yours, or if you have some secrets of your own to add, welcome aboard.

What do you who love an alcoholic/addict have in common? You hurt. You hurt a lot, whether it be the chronic ache as you watch someone you love slowly killing himself with alcohol, or the sudden blow when you discover that someone you love is an addict.

How do I know you hurt? Until four years ago, I was a troubled passenger, too, and as a troubled passenger, I had what you might call one of your longer cruises.

I was unhappy for twenty-four years, because my husband drank. Then he stopped drinking, and he began to change. He began to get better. I watched him stop drinking, and I began to change. I began to get worse. I got so bad that I was afraid I was going to die, and I had no idea why.

If you love a chemical dependent, practicing or recovering, and you find yourself growing increasingly uncomfortable, trying to make things better and somehow making them worse, your story is my story. Your suffering is my suffering. Your wounds are my wounds. I understand how you feel. I felt the same way. I felt the same way for so long that I thought that was the way I was supposed to feel, that life was meant to be uncomfortable and often downright miserable.

Well, I was wrong. And I'm going to show you how wrong I was. I'm going to share with you tools that I have learned and continue to learn, tools that make me grateful to be alive, tools that are helping me to experience serenity for the first time in my life, tools that help me to see that I am a part of the human race, no better and no worse, and, for the first time, to feel that I belong.

Will learning to use these tools restore a relationship? I don't know the answer to that question. But I *do* know that your relationship with the chemical dependent will not stay the same. It may begin again, it may come to an end, it may get better, or it may get worse, but willingness to use these tools *will* bring about a change.

The tools will seem simple. They're not. They are very hard to put to use. For one thing, they are tools for you, not somebody else. You've been so concerned about the alcoholic/addict that you may not know you *need* any tools to help you. If you know you do, you may not know where to find them. If you know where to find them, you may be afraid to ask for them.

You will feel that some of the tools do not apply to you. Read them anyway. There's always something more to learn.

You will also find yourself resisting much of what is said. That's perfectly natural. I did it all the time. All I ask is that you be *willing* to hear it. You will also forget what you are learning. I'm going to remind you many, many times. If you are an elephant, forgive me my excesses.

As you begin to work the tools, you may feel frustrated. Have compassion for yourself. You're probably not used to doing that.

Sometimes you'll hate yourself for doing what you did even though it was the best you could do. Sometimes you'll hate the chemical dependent for causing you all this hell in the first place.

You can learn to let go of hating yourself, and hating the alcoholic/addict. In fact, you can let go of hating to let go, and you'll be letting go with love.

Once you are willing to let go with love, you will be able to experience peace of mind and peace of heart, and all the hard work will have been worth it.

How do you learn to let go with love? Very slowly.

QUESTIONS

I don't know your answers, but I know your questions. I've had them, too. I thought a lot of mine were silly, but I learned that there aren't any silly questions. Many questions that you have may disappear as you continue to read. I try not to give advice, because I don't know *the* answers. There are no absolutes, but I hope that sharing the answers that have worked and continue to work for me will help you to find your own.

Q. *Your experience is with an alcoholic. Mine is with an addict. Aren't they two different problems?*

An alcoholic *is* an addict. The most widely used drug in the world is alcohol. The terms *alcoholic/addict, chem-*

ical dependent, user, and *substance abuser* are used inter-changeably throughout this book.

Q. *Your alcoholic is recovering. Mine is practicing. What good is this book going to do me?*

An alcoholic who is recovering is only one drink away from being a practicing alcoholic. That's the difference between our alcoholics. Whether *he* is dry or wet is not the problem. *Your* state of turmoil, *your* panic, *your* frustration, *your* insecurity, your everything, will prob-ably go on and on, just like mine did. You won't want to believe that. I didn't either. But I was forced to, once my husband found sobriety.

Q. *But the chemical dependent in your life is your husband. Mine is my son. How can* you *help* me?

It is true that the primary experiences throughout the book are wife/husband experiences, because they were my experiences. A lot of you reading the book will have very different ones and may feel that mine do not apply to you, but the underlying issues are in fact the same.

It doesn't matter whether the chemical dependent in your life is your spouse, child, parent, sibling, lover, or friend. They're all chemical dependents, and we're the ones who love them. You may hurt a little more here and I a little more there, but the tools are the same for all of us, because we're all in the same dilemma.

Q. *I don't know if this book is for me or not. I suspect that my daughter has a drug problem, but I'm not sure.*

You don't have to spend any more time trying to de-cide, nor do you have to wait for your daughter to acknowledge her addiction. Ask yourself these ques-tions: Is my daughter's using affecting my life? Do I spend time worrying about her, checking up on her, searching her room, watching her for signs of usage? If your answer is yes to any of these questions, this book is for you.

Q. *How do you know that the tools that work for you will work for me?*

There are no guarantees, but because we share common problems, we may share common solutions. And I'm not the only one to have been given these tools. They have been tried and tested by several million people. My experience with the tools will be different from somebody else's, just as your experience with the tools will be different from mine. But the tools themselves work for all of us.

Q. *What qualifies you to write this book?*

That's a very good question. I'm not a counselor, therapist, analyst, doctor, or any other kind of expert in the field of alcoholism/addiction. I qualify because I'm living proof that you don't have to be miserable if you love an alcoholic/addict, practicing or recovering. If *I* don't, *you* don't. Let me share these remarkable tools with you.

Okay. You and I are about to travel some stormy seas together. But they'll be no stormier than the ones you're on now.

The price of the ticket? Rigorous honesty.

The destination? As far as you choose to go.

What It Used to Be Like

Not Letting Go

The two most common questions:

If the user is using:
"How can I make him/her stop using?"

If the user is recovering:
"How can I make sure he/she doesn't use again?"

These two questions have the same answer, the only absolute answer in this book: You can't.

I wish I could give you the answer you want to hear. There's always a chance that I'm wrong. But what got me into such terrible trouble from the very beginning, and kept me there for so many years, was not believing that answer.

1

Life with a Practicing Alcoholic/Addict

THE FANTASY:
"ALL YOU NEED IS LOVE"

When we were first married, I noticed that my husband often drank what I thought was a little too much. But I wasn't terribly concerned. I was sure the situation would change. My love was going to change it.

Someday, it would go something like this:

Living room, 6:30 P.M. My husband is having his fourth martini. I'm fixing dinner in the kitchen, singing. All is merry.

"Dinner's ready, sweetheart."

"I'll have one more drink, dearest."

"Fine. I'll keep everything warm."

An hour later, I come in to him, lovingly. "Hungry yet?"

"Not quite. Just one more."

And I calmly go to the bar and pour all the liquor down the drain. "You don't need another drink. You have me."

He watches in grateful adoration. "Thanks, sweetie, for making me see the light."

He takes his fresh martini and pours it down the drain, then sweeps me into his arms and carries me to the bedroom, where we make passionate love. He never touches alcohol again.

This is not your situation? How about the following?

A June morning. A daughter, seventeen, who's graduating from high school today, is at the bathroom door. She sees her mother at the medicine chest with a bottle of pills.

"Ready, Mom?"

Her mother hides the pills behind her. The daughter knows what her mother is hiding.

The daughter hugs her mother and, with no hostility, says, "Mom, not today. You're going to take pictures. You want to be able to focus the camera, don't you?"

They both break up.

"Of course!" her mother says. "I completely forgot! Who needs this stuff, anyway?" And she flushes the pills down the toilet.

"Oh, Mom, I love you!"

And the mother goes happily to her daughter's graduation and never takes another chemical.

It's not a spouse or a parent who's the problem? It's a child, and children are different? Your love will definitely turn the tide.

A mother, holding an empty jewelry box, asks her husband, "What happened to all my jewelry? Do you suppose we've been burglarized?"

The son enters. "No, Mom and Dad. I stole it because I'd used up my allowance."

The father, putting his arm around his son: "Well, why didn't you just ask for more money?"

"Because I've been dealing again."

"We understand. You have a nasty habit. All kids your age have nasty habits."

"Yes, but I've been dishonest. I'll make it up to you. I promise."

The mother and father embrace him. "We love you."

"I know that, and that's why I'll never use the stuff again."

And the son remains clean for the rest of his natural life.

Not *your* situation? Okay, then, how about an unmarried couple living together? If love can fix anything, it can fix a lover.

A Sunday morning. Lovey, a young man, and Dovey, a young

woman, lie in bed. They're in an ecstatic mood.

Lovey speaks: "We had a wonderful time again last night."

"Did we?"

"You were hilarious. Again."

"Was I?"

Lovey's enjoying this. Lovingly, he says, "You kept telling the hostess that she looked just like your mother."

"I did?"

"You told her that through cocktails and dinner and during after-dinner drinks. You were so cute."

"Did the hostess think so?"

"Who cares about her?"

Lovey and Dovey laugh and hug.

Dovey gets serious now: "I wish I could remember how cute I was."

Lovey kisses Dovey and coos, "You can, sweetums. Just cut down."

Dovey looks at him adoringly. "Why didn't *I* think of that? From now on, no more after-dinner drinks."

"I love you."

And they get married and live happily ever after.

If any of these situations has happened in your home, you don't need this book. You've got it made. You're not living with an alcoholic/addict.

It would be wonderful if these scenes *could* happen. It would mean that our love could cure our loved one's addiction. But it can't. That's why these scenes are fantasies, and as much as we'd like to think otherwise, as we read them, we *know* they're fantasies. They're very easy to spot when they belong to someone else. But when they belong to us, we still believe that they're going to come true, and we keep trying to make them come true.

Q. *How do you know for sure that love won't cure a substance abuser?*

I don't know anything for sure, but, speaking from my own experience, if love could cure a substance abuser, my husband wouldn't have been drunk for twenty-four years.

Because love was the only tool I had, I used it a lot. I used it so much, I practically loved him to death. Not only didn't my love fix him, it almost killed *both* of us. But I didn't know that then and wouldn't have believed it if I had, because I was hell-bent on getting him sober and then keeping him that way. I didn't know that if he was going to get better, he would have to find his own tools. And I also didn't know that if I was going to get better, I would have to find my own tools. But he wasn't looking for help, and I didn't know I needed any, so we were in a fine pickle.

If you think your case is different, and your love will cure your user, keep trying. At some point, I think you'll begin to believe me. At least for that day, anyway. The next day, like me, you'll need reminding all over again.

In order to get to our first tool, we have to let go of the fantasy. How do we do that? By accepting the reality.

THE REALITY:
"WHAT'S LOVE GOT TO DO WITH IT?"

The scene with my husband as it actually happened:

Living room, 6:30 P.M. My husband is having his fourth martini. I'm fixing dinner, keeping one eye on my husband and one eye on my dried-out meat loaf. All is *not* merry.

"Dinner!!" I yell.

I get no response. I stomp into the living room with the dried-out meat loaf.

"I'm not calling you again. Look at this meat loaf. It looks like a meatball!"

"I didn't ask you to wait for me!"

"It's no fun eating alone every night!"

"Give me a chance to unwind!"

"You're on your fourth martini, and God knows how many you had before you came home."

"How else can I face *you*??"

"You're ruining my life. Day in and day out you—"

"Oh, go to hell!"

"No, *you* go to hell!"

My husband stomps out the door, and I throw the meat loaf at him.

"And don't come back!!"

I collapse to the floor in tears.

And he comes home, repentant, and we make up. The same scene happens again—and again—and again.

Why did I stay? How else could I fix him? As far as I was concerned, he was a good man who had a bad habit. Once he could learn to exercise some self-control, our problems would be over. So I became his mother, his nursemaid, his protector, and his shrink. Playing all those roles was a full-time job, even though I already had one.

Early on, I tried to reason with him. He was a reasonable man, except when he was drinking. But every time I tried to reason with him, he'd start drinking.

I decided that if he was going to drink like that, so would I. I'd show him! But after a few "his-and-her" martinis in public places, the shouting matches would begin. I'd make a hasty exit in tears, only to have to wait for him to pay the bill because I had no money with me to get home.

The fights were bad enough. The hangovers were unbearable. No, keeping up with him was clearly not the answer.

I know what—I'll pour out half the liquor in the bottle and substitute water. He drank twice as much.

Wait a minute. I've got it! I'll leave the office a half-hour earlier and serve dinner as soon as I hear his footsteps on the doorstep. That's the scene you just read. You can see how well it worked.

One day, he came home and announced that he was drinking no more hard liquor, only white wine. I was ecstatic. But not for long. It made no difference whatsoever. He could have switched to vanilla extract and the results would have been the same. Not only was his "drinking problem" not getting any better, it was getting worse. Alcohol is alcohol is alcohol.

Parties were a nightmare for me. *He* couldn't remember them. I did everything to "make nice," but I was embarrassed and ashamed, and I began to dread going to all social affairs.

He would promise that he'd had his last drink. And I would believe him, until he had his next drink.

I tried to keep the kids from knowing how much he drank, but the tension was beginning to show.

No more coaxing, no more cajoling, no more bribing. What did I find myself doing next? I found myself screaming at the top of my lungs.

I thought you were supposed to feel better after you let somebody have it, but I never did. Oh, maybe for thirty seconds, until the inner boomerang came back. Then I felt guilty, even though "I couldn't help it." "He *made* me act that way."

We had an actual fist fight, which was devastating to both of us.

I stuffed a handful of Seconal into my mouth one night, and threatened to swallow them if he took another drink. He took another drink, and I spit them into the toilet. I don't know why I didn't swallow them. I wanted to.

I could go on and on, but you get the picture. You're in your own picture.

I was in some kind of endless nightmare. My "real" life hadn't begun yet. This was only a dress rehearsal.

I had run out of new reactions. But the old ones were always there, and I used them more and more as he drank more and more.

QUESTIONS

Q. *Your story sounds a lot like mine, except that I'm going to give my husband an ultimatum. I've had it. Why didn't you do that?*

I did. Many times. In fact, he got so used to ultimatums that he paid no attention to them anymore. He saw through my empty threats, because that's what they were. There's nothing wrong with an ultimatum as long as it's your last one. But I seemed to have a limitless supply of final ultimatums.

The ultimatum you give your husband may indeed be your last one. But you may not feel tomorrow what you are feeling today. You may decide to change your mind, to give him "one more chance." If you do, don't beat yourself up for it. Have compassion for yourself. You're only human, and you're doing the best you can under very trying circumstances.

Q. *Should I try to force the abuser to join a program?*

Let's say you *are* able to force the abuser into a program. Can you stop her from using? I don't think so. That has to come from her. Getting her there is one thing. Keeping her clean is another.

An attempted "force" or two may not do any harm, and may actually "take," but only if she is ready to begin her recovery. If you continue to try, and she continues to fight, it may be a downhill battle for you. It can make things even worse. It can give her the excuse she's looking for to continue to use: "You're driving me to it." "You're trying to control me." "You won't leave me alone."

Q. *Should I keep on trying to cover up for my sister when she messes up?*

The words "keep on" imply that you have done a lot of covering up in the past. Did it do any good? When you take on somebody else's responsibility, you are taking it away from the person it belongs to. Your sister will never have to be responsible for things that are her responsibility—not as long as you keep taking care of them, which is exactly what she needs in order to continue to use. Is that what *you* need?

Q. *How can I make my husband cut down?*

You can't control the amount he uses. Neither can he. That's what makes him an alcoholic/addict.

Q. *I know my mother is an alcoholic. She doesn't. Should I tell her?*

You can tell her anything you like. What you can't do is control how your mother will react. As long as you don't expect something from your mother, you're free to do what you think is best for you.

If you do choose to tell her what you think, it might be better to tell her when she is sober. Try not to accuse her, if you can help it. She'll only get defensive.

Some people don't use the word *alcoholic* in confronting a loved one. Others do. Some use the words *drinking problem* because they feel that only an alcoholic can call himself an alcoholic. Still others talk about their own discomfort when the loved one drinks. Think about it. Try each one on for size and draw your own conclusions.

Q. *I know my son uses, but I am unable to say anything to him. I love him, and I'm afraid he'll turn against me. It's eating me up inside. What if he kills himself?*

Believe me, I understand how you feel. But it sounds to me as though *you* need help, too. You can make yourself sick by keeping it all in. You may have anger for your son that you don't want him to see. Take care of *you* first. Then you'll be better able to deal with your son.

You have to get those feelings out to someone. Can you and your spouse talk about it? Can you tell a friend you trust? How about a doctor or a minister? A therapist or counselor? If you know anyone you can talk to in a support-group program, that would be ideal. If you feel like yelling or crying, go ahead! Yell in front of your friend. Your friend won't care.

And you can talk to your son about your feelings. You simply can't *make* him change.

Q. *My daughter is an alcoholic/addict. She is completely irresponsible. She owes money to everybody. She's not paying her car insurance. She's about to be evicted. Should I pay her bills?*

It would be nice to think that if you paid her bills she would get better. But I've never seen that happen.

Look at me and my husband. I made excuses for him. I lied for him. I protected him. You can see where it got me.

I know you feel that your daughter is different because she is your child, but she isn't going to change any more than my husband did until she makes her own decision.

What I was doing is called "enabling." If you pay her bills, that's what you'll be doing, too.

Just what does "enabling" mean? When we enable, we are taking someone else's responsibility away from him or her. We are thus enabling that person to continue to be irresponsible. Your daughter's bills are *her* responsibility. Although you want to pay her bills in order to help her, you'd actually be doing her a disservice. How can she ever learn what her responsibilities are if you remove those responsibilities? Lying for someone, making excuses for someone, protecting someone—as I did with my husband—prevents that someone from having to take responsibility for his own actions. We call our chemical dependents irresponsible, because they are. But does our taking on their responsibilities make them less so?

Why do we enable? We do it because that's what we were brought up to believe we *should* do. We put up brave fronts; we keep the peace and the illusion of stability at all costs. We don't want our loved ones to have to suffer. And everybody who knows us tells us we're doing the best we can—and we are, because we don't know there's anything else we can do. But there is.

An addict will do anything to get a fix. Your daughter will promise this is the last time, she'll lie to you, she may even steal from you. That's how cunning her disease is.

Love her, don't enable her.

It isn't bad to say no.

Q. *But our son's underage. We're responsible for him. What are we supposed to do?*

You are legally responsible for him, but you are not responsible for his addiction. If he behaves badly, he must be responsible for what he does. It doesn't help to nag or scold your son. You can tell him that you love him but that you refuse to accept responsibility for his addiction.

Some good can even come from this. While denying your problems can create a wedge between you and your spouse, sharing them can bring you together. Be willing to hear each other and to offer each other comfort and support.

Q. *Do you mean that if my grandson comes to me and says he knows he needs help, I shouldn't help him?*

Not at all. "Helping" does not have to mean "enabling." Your grandson's acknowledgment that there is something wrong with him could be a first step toward his recovery, just as yours is. If he asks for the phone number of a support group or rehabilitation center, you can have one ready. But let *him* make the decision. And the call.

Q. *When my children ask questions about their dad, what can I tell them?*

You can tell your children that their father has a problem with his drinking and that he is ill. He can't help his illness, and he still loves them very much. Stress, too, that they did not cause his problem. Tell them that when he behaves in a strange way, it is a chemical that is causing that behavior. It is not something he wants to do.

Q. *I still don't see how you can help me. My mom was an addict and my dad an alcoholic while I was growing up. I'll never get over what they did to me. My life has been a nightmare from the beginning. How can your problems compare to mine?*

I know that your situation is not the same. You were damaged when you were a defenseless child. You may have far more fear of abandonment, far more rage, far more feelings of isolation, and you may be left with far more bitterness than I. But we are more alike than we are different. You need help just as I did, and do. You can't change the past, but you can begin to recover. It's never too late. I urge you to try the tools in this book. In addition, consider a support group like Al-Anon, Adult Children of Alcoholics, Nar-Anon, Cocanon, or Families Anonymous. There are no dues or fees, and you'll meet others who are experiencing the same feelings. Counseling and therapy are available, too. You may feel comfortable in a support group in conjunction with therapy. Choose what feels right for you.

Q. *How can I get my granddaughter into a recovery program?*

You can make the suggestion, but you can't control the outcome. When my husband found sobriety, he found it without my help.

Q. *I just found out that my daughter, who lives at home, has been doing drugs for two years. How could I have been so blind?*

It's possible that you knew there was something "different" about your daughter but weren't quite sure what it was. No one likes to accuse an innocent person.

It's possible you didn't *want* to know your daughter was doing drugs. What parent does?

It's also possible that your daughter was able to hide her drug abuse from you. Addicts can be superb liars. They know how to get what they want and to hide what they get.

You're not blind. You love an addict. Have compassion for both of you.

2

Life with a Recovering Alcoholic/Addict

THE FANTASY:
"UP, UP AND AWAY!"

"Once he/she stops using, we will walk arm in arm down the yellow brick road into the sunset, happily ever after."

I was utterly convinced that all my problems had come from my husband's drinking. Thus, all my problems would disappear once he stopped drinking. It sounded logical and seemed inevitable, but, to my complete surprise, it didn't work that way at all.

THE REALITY:
"WHAT GOES UP, MUST COME DOWN"

He did it all by himself.

I'll never forget the night my husband began his recovery. We had just been through another evening of "fun and games," and he went to bed at 7:00 P.M.—now his usual bedtime. I stomped into the bedroom, turned all the lights on, and lashed out once again. Once again, no response. I started to cry—sob is more like it—and sank to the floor. (I loved *drama*.) As I sat there, alone, in despair (I loved *self-pity*, too), I said, "I give up."

He got out of bed. I thought he was leaving me. Meekly, I asked, "Where are you going?"

"To a meeting."

"*What* meeting?"

"A.A."

"You're not an alcoholic!"

(When one doesn't want to know that one's loved one is an addict, one is considered to be "in denial." My response— "You're not an alcoholic!"—is a textbook example of denial. Of course, my husband had had "a little drinking problem" for twenty-four of the twenty-four years I'd known him, but that didn't make him an alcoholic!)

Thank God he ignored me.

He's been dry for five years.

Before you think I've given you the key to stopping your alcoholic/addict from using, I want you to know that I had said "I give up" many, many times before. And just as I was lying before, I was lying then. Only, at the height of the drama, I never knew I was lying. I only knew it when I stopped "giving up."

I spent the first year of my husband's sobriety waiting for my bliss to begin. I had at last gotten what I wanted. Well, almost. I was a little miffed that he got sober without my help, but no matter. He got sober. I waited—and waited. I watched *his* bliss begin. Where was mine?

Instead of bliss, I was feeling useless. He didn't need a mommy or nursemaid or shrink anymore. After twenty-four years of good, steady work—albeit without a salary—it was like a forced retirement.

But I wasn't ready to retire! I was ready to start living! As what? If I couldn't be a mommy or a nursemaid or a shrink, what was left? As far I was concerned, nothing.

What was I supposed to think about? My waking hours had been taken up with thoughts of how to cure him or of how to control how much he drank.

I knew who I was when he drank. I had no idea who I was when he got sober. I was lost, and I couldn't find *me*. I felt like I was attending a funeral—my own. I felt as though I were a cartoon figure, outlined in black but hollow in the middle.

Life is full of surprises. I expected to be filled with rejoicing. Instead, I was filled with emptiness.

But not for long. Soon, I began counting my husband's meetings instead of his drinks. If I felt he went to too few, I encouraged him to go to more. If he went to more, I complained that I was being neglected. I wasn't sure I liked his new friends. He said that this was okay with him, that I didn't have to like them. He was looking better than he had in years. He was feeling better, too. He would come home lighthearted, full of the joyous experience of the meeting, and my jaws would begin to shake from being clenched so tight. Who *was* this person? And, whoever he was, why wasn't he being punished for what he had done to me?

I wasn't thrilled with that desire for revenge, either. I began to feel guilty for having that desire. I could now add guilt to the old feelings of resentment, self-pity, anger, fear, self-righteousness, and lack of self-esteem, to name only a few. They were still locked up inside me, because I didn't know what to do with them. At that time I didn't even know what they were, but I knew they hurt. And they wouldn't go away.

At the end of his first year of sobriety, my husband went from good to better. I went from bad to worse.

What was going on here? I was feeling like a zombie. I started passing out in the supermarket. Not all the time, of course—only when I was well enough to get out of bed to go shopping.

I told no one what was happening to me. I was afraid to. What if they thought I was crazy?

What I didn't know then was that by the time my husband found a recovery program, I had become emotionally ill. And *his* recovery program wasn't going to make *me* emotionally well.

QUESTIONS

Q. *When my wife stopped using, I was ecstatic. Why weren't you? I don't understand your problem.*

I didn't understand my problem either, and I think it's great that you were able to respond in such a positive manner to your wife's finding a program. Perhaps you weren't as emotionally dependent upon her as I had become upon my husband. Not everyone responds in the same way. I urge you to keep reading, however.

I don't know how long your wife has been clean, but I, too, experienced enormous joy for the first few weeks of my husband's sobriety. It was like a honeymoon. It didn't last. *Your* joyous feelings may or may not last. I hope they do. But there is some reason you picked up this book, and although the degree to which you need help may be less than mine, you may still find whatever help you need here.

It's also possible that your wife will start using again. What would happen to your ecstasy then? I don't mean to be flippant, but I do want to point out that if your feelings depend upon your wife's behavior, there may be trouble ahead whether she is practicing *or* recovering.

Q. *My husband's in a program, too. I feel just as neglected as when he was using. When will he start to pay attention to me?*

When I start to get that feeling, I have to tell myself to let go of my self-pity and take some action. Feelings will follow. Perhaps if you weren't so dependent on him for your feelings in the first place, you wouldn't have to feel so neglected. What would make *you* feel good today? If you don't know the answer to that question, don't give up. Be tolerant with yourself as well as with your husband. And keep reading. There are tools that can help you.

Q. *Why does my wife have to go to so many meetings? Does she have to go forever? What kind of a life is that?*

Let's take one question at a time.

First, why so many meetings? Since your wife is a chemical dependent, her sobriety has to come first.

She is recovering, and in her recovery she is discovering that she has tools and is learning how to use them, just as you are about to do. This is a period of readjustment for both of you. Have patience. It will get better—better, perhaps, than you ever dreamed of.

Will she have to go to meetings forever? I'm afraid that's up to her. I know this is not the answer you want to hear, but if I said, "Two years and six months will do it," would you believe me? I think you can see how unanswerable this question really is.

Finally, what kind of a life is that? It's important to remember whose life we're talking about. She has her life, and you have yours. It might be more helpful if you could learn to simply live your own life, one day at a time, and let her live hers. That kind of freedom allows the two of you to grow together. Sharing your experiences with each other, listening to each other, and seeing the strength and hope you're both beginning to feel can do wonders for a relationship. Often, it works like a seesaw: when one is down the other is up, and the "up" one can support the "down" one. By *support*, I don't mean giving advice. Telling someone what to do doesn't seem to work. Listening can be support. Going about your own business can be support. Being there when help is asked for can be support.

You're both learning a new way of life. That takes time.

Q. *My daughter should "have it" by now! Hasn't she already learned whatever it is she was going to learn?*

A recovery program is a process, not an event. Your daughter is choosing to remain in recovery because her addiction can be arrested but never cured. We'll talk more about that later, but, speaking from my own experience, I need a constant reminder to use the tools

I've been given, or I'll forget to use them. I continue to learn from every meeting I go to. Maybe your daughter does, too.

Q. *My lover is recovering. Should I try to avoid places where alcohol is served?*

Talk it over. Maybe you'll both be more comfortable avoiding these places in the beginning. If it makes a difference to him but not to you, go with what he prefers. If you do go to a social affair where alcohol is served, and the host or hostess asks if either of you would care for a cocktail, don't answer for him. I remember piping up with, "No, he doesn't drink." My husband made it *very* clear that he would like me to mind my own business, and he was right. That kind of controlling can drive a drinker to drink. Especially a newcomer to sobriety. So bite your tongue!

Q. *What can I do about the discomfort I feel over my daughter's hanging around with addicts in the same recovery program?*

That's not unusual. First of all, you'll have to accept that your daughter is also an addict. Then, remember what your daughter was like before she found a program. She's in recovery now, just like the addicts she hangs around with. Lots of good things can come out of those relationships. They understand one another and can work with one another. Your daughter can't fool them the way she fooled you. They're "on to her." They've been through it.

Q. *My son goes to five Cocaine Anonymous meetings a week. Isn't he substituting one addiction for another?*

I can understand your frustration, but meetings are not addictive. Your son is consciously choosing these meetings to help him on his road to recovery. You sound very much like I did before I discovered that I needed my own support system.

If you still insist that meetings are addictive, are you willing to agree that they are a positive addiction? What is important is that your son is not using today.

What Happened
Learning to Let Go

After two years of feeling miserable, dreading my next anxiety attack, and growing more and more resentful as my husband was recovering, I knew that I had to do something. I couldn't live with these feelings any longer.

I had tried therapy, but I was afraid to reveal my feelings, so I spent a long time discussing my childhood. At that time I didn't really know what most of my feelings were, anyway. I was too ashamed and afraid to allow myself to know. So when the therapist asked me how I felt about this or that, more often than not I answered, "I don't know." And I honestly believed I didn't. I'm not saying that therapy was bad for me. It was probably exactly what I needed at the time. But the "floating anxieties" continued to float. I remember screaming in my car, "Go away! Stop driving me crazy! Get out of my life. I'm sick of you!" But the feelings remained.

I had hit bottom.

Hitting bottom is a term often used by alcoholics/addicts when they feel they can go no lower. One person's low may not appear to be as low as another's. But this makes no difference. The alcoholic/addict may have to hit bottom, whatever that may be, in order to be willing to admit to powerlessness over the chemical.

The expression is also often used by relatives and friends of the alcoholic/addict when they feel that they themselves can go no lower. And just as the alcoholic/addict may firmly believe that he has hit bottom, only to discover that he has still further to fall, so, too, can this happen to us. At least, it happened to me. I was sure that I had hit bottom.

I didn't know that I couldn't make the feelings go away. I didn't know that I had to first discover what they were, accept them, and be willing to let go of them slowly, one by one. And I certainly didn't know that there were tools available to help me along the way.

The process of letting go is a slow but direct result of learning to use the tools that the rest of this book will be dealing with. All the "stuff" that you're hanging on to, all the secrets that you are unwilling to reveal, all the feelings that are making you so unhappy can begin to disappear, one day at a time, if you are willing to work with the tools. You'll be confused at times, because only when you get all the pieces of the "letting go" puzzle together is the full picture available to you. Allow yourself to feel confused.

Occasionally, you'll also lose your patience. Learning to use the tools will require that you find it again. It may help you to learn not to equate "patience" with "self-control." Instead, think of patience as the letting go of self-will.

Will learning to use the tools make you happy forever? I doubt it. Pain is a part of life. But you will begin to feel better and to find some peace of mind. Coming from where I came from, that sounds like hitting the jackpot.

3

Finding the Tools and Going to Work
Letting Go of Handling It Alone

One day, when I had reached a new bottom but was still cling-
ing to my old life, I ran into a friend whose husband was still
drinking and who had recently discovered that her daughter
was doing drugs. My friend looked better than I'd ever seen her
look. How was this possible? My daughters were clean, my
husband was recovering, and I was having anxiety attacks in
supermarkets. I wanted to ask my friend what her secret was,
but I was afraid to. I didn't want her to know how bad off I was.

FRIEND: How are you?

ME: Fine.

FRIEND: Want to get some coffee?

ME: I'd love to, but I have to get home. (*Or else I'm going to
faint.*)

FRIEND: I don't think you're fine at all. You look like you're
about to pass out. (*She grabs my arm, leads me to her car, and
helps me in.*) Put your head between your knees. (*I do.*)
Do you get like this often?

ME: Only in supermarkets.

FRIEND: Are you anxious about something?

ME: What's to feel anxious about? My husband's terrific.

FRIEND: Are *you*?

ME: There's nothing wrong with me. (*My head is between my
knees, and I'm gasping for air.*)

FRIEND: Are you sure? You lived with a practicing alcoholic for
twenty-four years.

ME: *You* still *do*, for God's sake! How come *you* aren't passing
out in supermarkets?

FRIEND: I never did that. But I threw up a lot on busses.

ME: What was wrong with you?

FRIEND: The same thing that's wrong with you.

ME: How come you're not still throwing up?

FRIEND: I stopped taking busses. No, I'm kidding. I'm getting help.

ME: (*Time to get away.*) Yeah, well, thanks for letting me use your front seat.

FRIEND: Want to get help where I'm getting help?

ME: You don't need help. You look great!

FRIEND: That's because I'm getting help. I found a fellowship for relatives and friends of alcoholics, called Al-Anon.

ME: Oh, God.

FRIEND: Have you heard of it?

ME: Of course. Al-Anon, Nar-Anon, Cocanon. Soon there'll be Uppers-, Downers-, and In-Betweeners-Anon. . . .

FRIEND: Want to try it?

ME: Why should *I* be punished for what *he* did?

FRIEND: What makes you think it's a punishment?

ME: *He* was the sick one, not me!

Silence.

ME: (*Time for a little honesty here.*) Listen, I think I'll leave the religious stuff to you.

FRIEND: It's not a religious program.

ME: Look, I don't want to be flip about this. I know you're going through a lot with your family, and clearly Al-Anon is working for you. I mean, your husband's still drinking, and your daughter . . . Maybe if I'd known about it when *my* husband was still drinking . . . but I certainly don't need it now.

Six months passed. Freeways started making me dizzy.

I knew at last what "bottom" was. I couldn't live the way I had been living anymore. I had to have help. But I was too ashamed to admit to myself that I needed it, and too afraid to let anyone else know I needed it.

Then I ran into my friend again, this time when I was stopped on the shoulder of the freeway. She recognized my car.

FRIEND: Can I call Triple-A for you?
ME: There's nothing wrong with my car.
FRIEND: (*getting it*) Need a lift?

Then, in her car, on the way home:

FRIEND: I'm going to a meeting tonight. Would you like me to pick you up?
ME: If you want me to be there.

Later, as we were driving to the meeting:

ME: I really feel silly.
FRIEND: How come?
ME: Because he's *sober*!
FRIEND: You'll meet a lot of people like you. Not everybody's relatives and friends are still practicing.
ME: What if I meet somebody I know?
FRIEND: It's an anonymous program. Only first names are used.
ME: Yeah, but if I know *them*, they know *me*.
FRIEND: We're all playing in the same band.
ME: What do you have to do?
FRIEND: Nothing.
ME: You sit there and do nothing??
FRIEND: You share, if you want to.
ME: Share what?
FRIEND: Whatever you choose to share.
ME: I *don't*.
FRIEND: That's fine.
ME: Look, maybe I shouldn't go.
FRIEND: All right. Do you want to wait at a coffee shop for me? I'll only be an hour and a half.
ME: Wait for an hour and a half alone?
FRIEND: I'd give you my car, but. . . .

She had me.

ME: What do people talk about?

FRIEND: All kinds of things. If they have a problem, they may choose to share that.

ME: You keep saying "share" this, "share" that. Don't you just talk?

FRIEND: Yes, but you say what you have to say. Nobody interrupts you.

ME: So people just sit and complain about their alcoholics.

FRIEND: In the beginning, some do. But after a while, as people begin to recover. . .

ME: What do you mean, "recover"? You're in the wrong program, aren't you?

FRIEND: No. Alcoholism affects all of us.

ME: Well, I'm not sick.

FRIEND: Okay. After a while, people who have spent more time in the program share what it used to be like, or what it's like now, or how the program has helped them to become stronger, or—listen, I suddenly feel like I'm preaching. See for yourself what we share. I can't re-create a meeting for you. All I can tell you is that you'll hear a lot of experiences like yours. I'm not going to promote it. Maybe you'll be attracted enough to it to give it a whirl.

Silence. Then I decide to really get to it:

ME: Well, I'm not going to become a true believer.

FRIEND: Relax. You don't have to become anything. I was scared just like you, until I realized I had nothing to lose except my misery.

I went to my first meeting for three reasons:

3. I didn't want to wait for her.
2. I was ashamed to take a cab home.
1. My friend had what I wanted.

I walked in with glazed, unblinking eyes. Oh, God, what if someone saw what I was feeling? I was so afraid.

There were about twenty women and men, and they were

drinking coffee and laughing. I couldn't imagine *what* they had to laugh about. They were warm to me and to the other two newcomers, who looked as lost and frightened as I felt. I was relieved they were there.

I don't remember a lot about that meeting. I do remember that I didn't "share." Some of what was shared sounded like what I had been through or what I was going through, only in many cases it sounded worse. I couldn't believe that these people were so willingly divulging all the same feelings I was hiding. And that they were able to laugh about them—and to cry about them.

There was a "leader" who ran the meeting and acknowledged the raised hands, one at a time. He was only the leader for that night. The next week somebody else would do it.

When it was over, a woman came up to me. She shook my hand and said she understood my reluctance to share. She said it had taken her a long time to share. She'd been afraid she'd make a fool of herself, and what had helped her find the courage was getting a sponsor.

ME: What's a sponsor?

WOMAN: Well, it's somebody who can help you on a one-to-one basis. After a few meetings, you'll find yourself having more feelings in common with one person than another. Your experiences will probably be more alike than different. You may find yourself nodding yes a lot when she shares. She will have spent more time in the program than you. When that happens—

ME: Yeah, well, look, I'm not ready to get a sponsor. I don't even know if I'm coming back, so—

WOMAN: (*smiling*) It took me a year to come back to my second meeting, and another year to get a sponsor. I really do understand. I hope it doesn't take you that long.

The next week, I went back. I figured, what the hell? It was free, the coffee wasn't bad, my husband was at his own meeting, and my daughters had their friends. I had no place else to go.

Three months later, I went up to the woman who had come

up to me at the first meeting, and I asked her to be my sponsor. She said yes.

ME: You don't know what you're letting yourself in for.
NEW SPONSOR: Neither do you.

4

Whose Disease Is It, Anyway?

Letting Go of Old Beliefs

Because I had created my own picture of what A.A. meetings were like without ever having gone to one, my sponsor suggested that I go to some. I asked my husband if he would mind if I went with him to one of his "open" meetings (that is, not restricted to alcoholics). He said it would be fine. I arranged to meet him there. When I walked in, I expected to see a bunch of skid-row bums and my husband sitting there. I couldn't have been further off the mark. There were men and women of all ages, laughing and talking and acting very "normal." In fact, it was a lot like *my* meetings.

I heard somebody at the meeting share that alcoholism is a physical compulsion coupled with a mental obsession. I could believe that, but I still didn't think it was a disease.

SPONSOR: Do you still think it's only a bad habit?
ME: I don't see what difference it makes what I think.
SPONSOR: Then try acting "as if."
ME: As if *what*?
SPONSOR: As if you believe it's a disease.
ME: Why? Why do I have to do that?
SPONSOR: You don't *have* to do anything. My sponsor suggested it to me, and it helped me.
ME: Why?
SPONSOR: Because when I looked at my husband's alcoholism

as nothing more than a bad habit, I blamed him and belittled him. When I was able to look at it as if it were a disease, I could feel a little understanding and compassion. The more willing I am to believe what the experts say, the more my understanding and compassion grow. But I had to let go of the "bad-habit" belief first.

ME: But my husband's cured! What difference does it make what I thought he had?

SPONSOR: Practicing or recovering, your husband has a disease that *can't* be cured. The disease doesn't go away when the bottle does. It's merely arrested. It's very similar to diabetes. Do you believe that diabetes is a disease?

ME: Of course.

SPONSOR: What if your husband had diabetes?

ME: He doesn't.

SPONSOR: Can you act as if he did?

ME: I don't want to pretend.

SPONSOR: You pretended for a lot of years that he wasn't an alcoholic.

ME: I'm through pretending.

SPONSOR: The A.M.A. has accepted alcoholism as a disease since 1956. In 1970, *The New England Journal of Medicine* published an article—

ME: I'm sorry. Maybe some alcoholics have a disease, but I don't believe my husband does.

SPONSOR: Why not?

ME: (*letting out anger I didn't even know was there*) Because if it's a disease, that lets him off the hook! I want him to be punished for what he did to me!

And, to my surprise, I found myself crying. She didn't try to stop me.

SPONSOR: If you think of your husband as having only a bad habit, what does that make you feel toward him?

ME: Resentment.

SPONSOR: If you think of your husband as having a disease, what does *that* make you feel toward him?

ME: Compassion.

SPONSOR: Which one feels better?

ME: Believing he has a disease.

SPONSOR: Are you willing to believe he has a disease?

ME: I am, for now.

SPONSOR: Great. When you're not, try acting as if you believe it anyway, until you really do. Okay?

ME: I'll try.

Then, a few weeks later:

ME: I'm beginning to be civil to my husband.

SPONSOR: Good.

ME: Yes, but he still drives me up the wall. He has the same disapproving looks that he had when he was drinking, and he lapses into the same silences, and he takes forever to answer one little question I ask, and he still—

SPONSOR: Hold it! First of all, just because your husband doesn't drink doesn't mean he's not the same person. And what's more important, what your husband does or doesn't do is not why you're here. What's going on with *you*?

ME: Well, I'm still avoiding freeways and markets. But I figure those things will go away in time, as my husband changes.

SPONSOR: Your husband is responsible for *your* anxiety?

ME: Well, I wouldn't have gotten this way if he hadn't had the disease.

SPONSOR: So what does that tell you about the disease?

ME: (*as a joke*) That it's contagious.

SPONSOR: That's a terrific way of putting it.

ME: I didn't catch his need to drink!

SPONSOR: No. You didn't catch his physical compulsion. What *did* you catch?

ME: I have no idea.

SPONSOR: How about his mental obsession?

ME: I was never mentally obsessed with booze!

SPONSOR: What *were* you mentally obsessed with?

ME: I don't know.

SPONSOR: What time did he go to bed when he drank?

ME: (*responding like a robot*) 7:00 P.M.

SPONSOR: How many martinis did he have before dinner?

ME: On a good night, three.

SPONSOR: What did he drink after dinner?

ME: Rémy Martin on the rocks with a twist.

SPONSOR: When did he find sobriety?

ME: August 8, 1980.

SPONSOR: How many meetings does he go to a week?

ME: Two now, on Mondays and Thursdays. For the first six months, it was five.

> *My sponsor took a deep breath and waited. I began to shake my head no, back and forth.*

ME: Oh . . . my . . . God. My husband is my drug. I'm addicted to the addict.

I wasn't able to laugh *or* cry. I was only able to sit in this wash of realization. *I* was ill. Whatever happened with my husband, it was time for me to get to work on my own recovery.

"My wife's in a program, and I hate her new friends. What should I do?"

"My daughter is as much a stranger to me in recovery as she was when she was practicing. What's going on with her?"

"When will my son apologize for the harm he's caused us?"

"How do I know for sure that my husband's not still using?"

"My mother won't tell me what goes on at those meetings. Why won't she let me go to one with her?"

All of these questions have one thing in common. They are perfect illustrations of a loved one's addiction to the addict.

It's time for *all* of us to get to work on our own recovery.

My sponsor made a suggestion to me.

SPONSOR: You may find some of this rough going. Worth it, but rough going. I'm going to give you an easy exercise to start out with. I'd like you to think of three "gratefuls."

ME: What are those?

SPONSOR: Three things in your life that you're grateful for.

ME: What's easy about that? Offhand, I can't think of anything.

Silence.

SPONSOR: How about your daughters?

ME: Of course.

SPONSOR: What else?

ME: I'm grateful that I live close to the ocean.

SPONSOR: Great. One more.

ME: (*This was tough.*) My firm mattress.

SPONSOR: There you go. The first thing I'd like you to do is get a journal and list three "gratefuls" in it every night.

ME: Write them down? Every night?

SPONSOR: Uh-huh.

ME: How long do I have to keep writing them down?

SPONSOR: Until you *want* to write them down.

ME: Why?

SPONSOR: So you can see how many things you have to be grateful for. Otherwise you might forget. I did, when I was a newcomer.

ME: Okay, I guess I can do that.

SPONSOR: Then I'd like you to list three "did wells."

ME: What are they?

SPONSOR: Three things you did well that day.

ME: I think I can handle the "gratefuls," but I don't know about the "did wells." What's the point?

SPONSOR: So you can see how many things you did well. Otherwise, you'll forget those, too. Especially on bad days.

ME: But why do I have to write all this down?

SPONSOR: Because it will help you to see them. If you just list them in your mind, they'll disappear. I want you to be able to *look* at them.

ME: Can I repeat some?

SPONSOR: Yes, if you did them well *that day*.

ME: I don't know about all this writing.

SPONSOR: I told you that you might find some of this rough going, remember? Well, seeing good healthy things about yourself will help you along the way. And, by the way, we've only just begun. I suggest you use a three-ring notebook so that you can keep adding to it.

So I went to work on my "gratefuls" and "did wells." I've used "brushed my teeth" a lot on *both* lists when I've been desperate.

But I still do it, and it does help. So, get a notebook. Each evening, write down three "gratefuls" and three "did wells," and be sure to date each entry. In doing this, you'll begin to be able to *see* your growth, your changes.

REVIEW

Q. *Review what? I haven't learned anything yet!*

I'm sure that's true for many of you. For those of you who know little or nothing about alcoholism/addiction, however, now is the time to get informed, by reading about the disease or by going to some open Alcoholics Anonymous, Cocaine Anonymous, or Narcotics Anonymous meetings. If the substance abuser in your life is not in a program of recovery, go anyway. And if the substance abuser *is* in a program, go as well.

Q. *Is it all right to go to a meeting with the substance abuser?*

Yes, if it's all right with him. Otherwise, go alone or with a friend. Don't make it an issue. Who you go with isn't important.

Q. *My wife is still drinking. Should I tell her I'm going?*

That's up to you, but it's not necessary. What *is* important is that you not try to force her into a program of her own or leave the literature you're reading on her pillow.

You can do these things, of course. You can do anything you please, but you may be in for a big letdown if your scheme backfires. You can't control the outcome.

Addicts are like everybody else. They don't like to be told something they don't want to hear. If she asks you, go ahead and show her, go ahead and tell her. But you can't *make* her use your tools, just as I can't make you use mine.

Q. *Why should I go or read or do any of this?*

So you can begin to rid yourself of the blame and the belittling you felt toward the user. Why should you do that? Because these feelings may be keeping you from getting better.

I hope that the effect someone else's addiction has had on you is clearer to you now. This effect is why addiction is called "the family disease."

Someone else's addiction did not cause your problems. It aggravated and magnified the problems you already had. You probably won't believe that. I didn't.

Perhaps an example will help to convince you.

Long before I met my husband, one of my problems was my need to play the role of "nurse" to others. I thought I knew what was best for them, that I could fix them, make them better. Until my husband came along, I didn't have much of a chance to play that role. His disease allowed me to major in nursing. My nursing tendency flourished and became inappropriate behavior.

So far, what's in your tool kit that you are at least *willing* to try?

1. Alcoholism/addiction is a disease.
2. You, too, are ill.

5

The "Yes, But/No, But" Game

Letting Go of Power You Never Had

In trying to fix my husband—and, although I hate to admit it, everyone else I loved, because I thought everyone else I loved needed fixing—I believed I had the power to do the fixing. I don't know why I believed that. I had no evidence to support that belief, but that's what I believed, nevertheless. What I didn't know was that I was trying to do the impossible, because I didn't have the power I thought I had. I will never have the power I thought I had. And on good days, that's a "grateful."

But that doesn't stop me from believing I still have the power to do the fixing, sometimes. Old beliefs are hard to get rid of.

It's funny, but my efforts at controlling my husband, my family, and my closest friends grew in direct proportion to the extent that I failed.

I had *never* succeeded in my efforts to control others, except when my children were babies and needed my control in order to survive—but was that really control? Could I ever "make" them sleep through the night? Could I ever "make" them eat their strained liver? Could I ever "make" them stop crying? No, that wasn't control, either. That was simply *my* will clashing with theirs.

Even when I thought I had control, I soon found out I didn't. There *are* no exceptions, but that didn't stop me from trying. I tried so hard I became ill.

I became obsessed with trying to control my husband's drinking. When he got sober, did I stop trying to control his drinking? Of course. But now I tried to control his sobriety, while worrying that he might have a slip.

When I was a newcomer, I heard people talk about being "powerless." I hated the thought. It was humiliating. To admit to being powerless meant admitting that I was a failure. To acknowledge powerlessness meant surrendering my control. It meant accepting the fact that I had no control over anyone. I didn't buy it.

SPONSOR: Didn't your husband find the program when you stopped trying to manipulate him?

ME: Yes, but—

SPONSOR: Didn't you fail every time you tried?

ME: Yes, but—

SPONSOR: Didn't you tell me he was now leading a much better life without your telling him how to do it?

ME: Yes, but—

SPONSOR: Didn't others in the program share the same experiences with their loved ones who were still using?

ME: Yes, but—(*I loved playing "Yes, but."*)

SPONSOR: Did you ever have any power over your husband?

ME: No, but—(*Aha! A new game!*)

SPONSOR: Do you have any power over him now?

ME: No, but—

SPONSOR: Has anything happened to make you think you will have power over him?

ME: No, but—

SPONSOR: Then can you accept the fact that you are powerless over your husband?

ME: No! (*I was getting tired of this game now.*)

SPONSOR: Why not?

ME: Because I can't!

SPONSOR: Are you willing to substitute *won't* for *can't*?

I refused to answer. I didn't like her anymore.

SPONSOR: You've admitted you never had, do not have, and

never will have any power over your husband. What does that make you?

ME: Powerless.

SPONSOR: Are you willing to let go of that power?

ME: I don't know how to do it.

SPONSOR: You don't have to *do* anything. Can you simply be *willing*?

ME: How can I be willing?

SPONSOR: By letting go of being *un*willing.

There was a long pause here. I don't give up easily. Neither does she.

SPONSOR: Are you willing to let go of the power *you don't have*?

To let go of something that was never mine in the first place? *That* struck home. I began to laugh. I laughed so hard I began to cry. I had never felt such a sense of relief. We hugged each other. I was powerless, and I would always be powerless.

The next day, I'd forgotten I didn't have any power.

I forget that I am powerless because I don't want to believe that I am. I have to keep reminding myself one day at a time. Of course, the best reminder for me is trying to exercise the power I don't have. That reminds me I am powerless. On bad days, I pay no attention to the reminder and must "act as if" I were powerless until it finally sinks in.

Why is it that rats can learn which tunnels lead to the cheese, but I can't? I keep going down tunnels where the cheese *isn't*, just as you may.

Perhaps you're still not convinced. You're thinking that I wasn't clever enough with my husband, and that you *will* be clever enough with your wife. That I didn't hold on to the purse strings, but that you do with your son. That I didn't understand my husband as well as you understand your mother. And, of course, you may be right. There are lots of tunnels out there. If you find one that leads to the cheese, send me a map.

QUESTIONS

Q. *I know I'm powerless over my husband, but he's had three slips in his first year of sobriety, and each one has felt like a mortal wound. How can I stop this constant terror I have that his next slip won't be a temporary one?*

Knowing that you're powerless is only the beginning. Believing it takes a little more time. Your terror can be temporary if you are willing to continue to work on your own recovery.

As for your husband, he's in recovery, too. He's trying. Slips are not uncommon. He has a very good chance of making it.

I suggest that you find yourself a support group, just as he did, and share your feelings of terror with others, not with your husband. He needs your support.

Q. *It's so easy for you to sit there and talk about powerlessness over your husband. You didn't bring him into the world. He's not fifteen! If anything bad happens to my daughter, I'll blame myself. And the whole world will blame me, because I failed to teach her properly. I'm responsible! How can I live with those feelings?*

You are forgetting: she has a disease. You didn't cause it. You can't control it. You can't cure it. Would you blame yourself if she had leukemia? I don't think so. There *is* no blame with a disease.

As for the rest of the world's blaming you, might that not be your creation? Is it possible that you blame other parents whose children are addicts and are therefore afraid that *they* blame *you*? Join a support group like Families Anonymous. All blame and shame can disappear and be replaced by compassion.

If you still refuse to believe that your daughter has a disease, here's where "acting as if" can help you enormously. Try it the next time you look at her. If it doesn't work the first time, try it again. Be patient with yourself and with your daughter.

Q. *I really understand powerlessness when I read about it, but then my son comes home stoned and the understanding goes away. How can I keep it?*

What a wonderful question! It's about you, not your son. You may not know this, but that's one of the first signs your own wellness is beginning.

When your son comes home stoned, try backing off. You won't want to. Neither do I, when things aren't going the way I *want* them to. I go on a self-will bender. Then backing off is the first step I must take in order to let go of the power I don't have anyway.

How do you back off? Take a walk. Call a friend. Talk about something else, anything else. Get your eyes off your son, without punishing him with your silent scorn. You don't have time for scorn, anyway. You have your own homework to do. How about rereading this chapter on powerlessness?

You'll find more help if you continue. Easy does it.

Q. *My daughter is twenty years old, and she's killing herself. I think she wants to die, and that's killing us! Sometimes, God forgive me, I wish she would die. It would all be over then. I don't know this stranger. She threatens us. If we refuse to give her money, she steals it. Honest to God, I think I hate my own child. I know I've failed somewhere, but I don't know where. You don't know what it feels like. How can you compare your problems with a husband to mine with a child?*

It's true that a husband is not a child. A parent's sense of responsibility is much greater. I could have left at any time.

But our feelings are not far apart. The resentment you feel for your daughter is the same resentment I felt for my husband. There were times when I wished he were dead, too, because I felt he was ruining not only my life but our children's lives as well. And I felt that I had failed because I couldn't find the key to make him stop drinking.

Whatever you're going through, others have been through, and many have been through worse.

I've seen a mother shed tears over a teenage son who had just died from an overdose. Her tears were full of rage against him, and against herself for not having saved his life.

A young woman breaks down because her mother's brain has been destroyed by alcohol.

A father is called to the police station and finds that his young son has stolen the family car, driven it while under the influence, run down a pedestrian, and is now being held for homicide.

An attempted suicide brings a newcomer to the program. She has an alcoholic husband, two addicted children, and an alcoholic mother and grandfather. I wouldn't believe it on a soap opera, yet it's true.

Just when we feel that our experience is the worst, we find that we "ain't heard nothin' yet." That's one of the reasons the program works so well. Whatever we share, we know that others have been through the same or worse. If we can begin to live again, so can you.

And believe me, we can. I've seen people who could do nothing but cry begin to laugh. And I've seen others who could *not* cry be able to let go of their grief. That's the strength we get out of sharing and hearing others share. That's the hope we begin to feel together.

Q. *What if my daughter takes an overdose?*

You did not *cause* and you cannot *control* or *cure* the disease of addiction. You can give your daughter phone numbers where she can find help. You can try an intervention program. You can give her money. You can stop giving her money. You can scream at her, and you can refuse to talk to her. You can love her with all your heart, and sooner or later you will discover that love is not enough to conquer this terrible disease. No matter what you do, you can't make her stop using. Only she can do that. You can pave the way, you can make suggestions, you can force her into a recovery program, you can hold her hand, you can threaten, coax, cajole, and bribe, but *you cannot make her stop using.* You are powerless. You are powerless. You are powerless.

Q. *But how can I ever stop blaming myself?*

Forgive me, but whether she does or doesn't o.d., the tools can help you. I've felt their help and seen them help others. The bereaved mother is getting through the pain of losing her son. She'll never forget, but she uses tools to buoy her. The daughter is finding a parachute to break her fall as she watches her mother go mad. Through the tools, the father is learning what his responsibilities are and what they aren't. He is able to stop blaming his son and himself. The newcomer is no longer suicidal. She is learning to get on with her *own* life. That's what we're *all* doing, because ours are the only lives we can get on with.

If you don't believe me, you can continue to bail her out or pay her rent. But you are not necessarily helping her by doing so. In fact, you may be doing just the opposite. She is not a baby anymore. She is old enough to own responsibilities. They rightfully belong to her. If you take them away, you are taking away what are hers. This may *enable* her to continue to use. I know you want just the opposite to happen, but you cannot control what is not yours. *Her* addiction belongs to her.

You may have reached the point where you know intellectually that you are powerless, but you still don't *feel* it. Don't give up. Try to *be* powerful with your daughter. After you have tried—and tried—and tried to be powerful with your daughter, you will eventually come to feel as well as know that you are powerless.

Since you are powerless over what she does or does not do, can you accept her as she is? If your answer is "I can't!" try "I won't!" You are resisting being powerless because you don't want to be. That's perfectly natural, but it isn't helping you or your daughter.

6

Taking the Load Off
Letting Go of Playing God

As I continued to go to meetings, I heard more people share about "a higher power." I was very uncomfortable. It was amazing to me that these intelligent people constantly referred to a "God as they understood him" or "a power greater than themselves" and that they had no embarrassment in sharing this. Maybe they weren't as smart as I thought they were.

I must add here that not all newcomers are like I was. Many have strong spiritual beliefs already, so they are not troubled by this kind of sharing. But for me, it put the whole program under a cloud.

For a long time, I took consolation in the words read at every meeting: "Take what you want and leave the rest." I was able to leave that stuff behind.

My sponsor explained that the tools in Anonymous programs were spiritual ones, and if I wanted to work them with her, I might have to do some exploring. (Oh, no! Here it comes.) She had been like me in the beginning, she said. She used to feel physically ill when people talked about a higher power. Good. I wasn't alone.

SPONSOR: Do you believe there is anything greater than you are?
ME: Of course. Lots of things.
SPONSOR: Can you choose one *specific* power greater than you?
ME: What kind of power?
SPONSOR: Any power you choose.
ME: A he, a she, or an it?
SPONSOR: It's your choice.
ME: I don't believe in God.

SPONSOR: All right.

ME: I don't believe in heaven or hell.

SPONSOR: Fine.

ME: I don't think I belong here. I don't believe in anything. I'm not a religious person.

SPONSOR: It's not a religious program. It's a spiritual one.

ME: I'm not spiritual, either.

SPONSOR: Okay.

She waited, and so did I. But I got uncomfortable with the silence.

ME: So I'm supposed to choose a power greater than I am?

SPONSOR: A specific one.

Nothing came to my mind at all. Nothing except resistance. She waited, and so did I, once again.

SPONSOR: All right. Why don't you go home and write about your resistance?

ME: What resistance? I just can't think of anything.

SPONSOR: Didn't you say that you believed there were lots of things greater than you?

ME: Sure.

SPONSOR: Can you name one?

ME: Nothing comes to mind.

SPONSOR: Go home and write about why nothing comes to mind.

I did not want to do that. I was getting tired of writing down all those "gratefuls" and "did wells." I had to come up with an answer, fast.

ME: The ocean!

SPONSOR: Great. Go home and write about what the ocean makes you feel.

I drove to the ocean early one morning. As I walked along the shore, I felt very peaceful. I always do when I walk along the shore. I have enormous respect for the ocean. I love everything about it.

I stopped walking, closed my eyes, and let myself feel what I loved—the smell, the sound of the waves, the breeze that is always there, the sand under my feet, the colors, the size, the timelessness of it all. I felt an overwhelming sense of gratitude that it was there and that I was there.

And I knew I would never have any power over it at all. I was glad, because I didn't want any. The ocean was not my responsibility. What a relief.

SPONSOR: What would you call that experience you had?

ME: A good one.

SPONSOR: Would you call it a spiritual one?

I knew I had felt something I would never intellectually understand.

ME: *Yes, but—*

SPONSOR: Are you willing to choose the ocean as a power greater than yourself?

ME: *Yes, but—*

And we laughed. But I wasn't willing to let go completely. As usual.

ME: What if I change my mind tomorrow?

SPONSOR: Then you can change your higher power. No decision has to be forever.

ME: But why do I have to believe in a higher power?

SPONSOR: You don't have to. But, in my experience, being willing to believe in a higher power—in God as I understand him—gives me serenity.

ME: Yeah, well, I *don't* understand him. By the way, what do I do with this "spiritual experience"?

SPONSOR: Let yourself experience it.

She kept life so simple.

QUESTION

Q. *I have the same resistance that you do to anything spiritual. Will the tools not work for me?*

I don't think there's a yes or no answer to that question. If you keep in mind that you, too, need help, as does the addict in your life, and if you stay open to what comes up for you, you'll find an answer that works for you. For me it's essential to believe in a power greater than myself, whatever it may be and however it may change, because otherwise I'll take on responsibility that doesn't belong to me.

7

Where the Power Is
Letting Go of Feeling Trapped

By letting go of the power I didn't have, one day at a time, I slowly began to discover the power I *did* have and never knew I had and, in the beginning, didn't even want. What am I talking about?

I wanted power (control) over my husband, my family, and my friends. I wanted to exercise *my* will over theirs. Never mind that I never got what I wanted. I wanted it anyway. And the desire for power became so strong that it became an obsession.

Why was I unwilling to let go of that obsession? Or, to put it another way: Why did I insist on hanging on to that obsession?

One very important reason was that obsessing on another kept my eyes on him or her and off the one I had the power to do something about. Me. But I didn't know I had the power to take my eyes off another and take a look at myself. I thought I had to keep trying to change other people. After all, they needed changing, and if *I* didn't keep trying to change them, who would? It never occurred to me that just as I am my responsibility, so, too, are they theirs.

As the obsession diminished, I began to focus on the changes I *was* free to make. Changes in me. And oh, I did not want to change my own behavior. I was so used to it. But I had no choice, once I was able to see the choices I had.

In the program, I was beginning to grow. Frightened as I often was, there was no turning back. Painful? Sometimes. Would I like to return to what I was? No.

What is the power I have over myself? I have the power to choose. I have options. Difficult as they are to exercise, I can't *not* see them anymore—even when I'd rather not—because I know they're there.

I think it's time to show you an example.

Here again is the "Reality" scene you've read before. Only this time take your eyes off my husband and look at *my* behavior.

Living room, 6:30 P.M. My husband is having his fourth martini. I'm fixing dinner, keeping one eye on my husband and one eye on my dried-out meat loaf. All is *not* merry.

"Dinner!!"

I get no response. I stomp into the living room with the dried-out meat loaf.

"I'm not calling you again. Look at this meat loaf. It looks like a meatball!"

"I didn't ask you to wait for me!"

"It's no fun eating alone every night!"

"Give me a chance to unwind!"

"You're on your fourth martini, and God knows how many you had before you came home."

"How else can I face *you*??"

"You're ruining my life. Day in and day out—"

"Oh, go to hell!"

"No, *you* go to hell!"

My husband stomps out the door, and I throw the meat loaf at him.

"And don't come back!!"

I collapse to the floor in tears.

And he comes home, repentant, and we make up. The same scene happens again—and again—and again.

Did you take a good look at what I was doing, and that I didn't know I was doing? For one thing, I was talking to a person whose mind had been altered by a chemical. Was I talking to a rational person? Hardly. I was talking to a chemical, and a chemical can't hear me, no matter how loudly I scream. So who ends up frustrated and angry? The chemical? No. Me. Was *I* a rational person? No, but *I didn't know I had a choice* about my actions and reactions.

Today, I know I do.

When I wasn't screaming, I found myself being self-right-eously silent. I tightened my jaw and sighed heavily so my husband would see how much I was suffering and would feel guilty. But, again, I was punishing a chemical. I sat there feeling sorry for myself, and he continued to drink. *I didn't know I had a choice.*

Today, I know I do.

What was waiting at the end of each of my tunnels? Failure. Did that stop me from plunging headlong into another? No, because I didn't know I could do anything else. What feelings did failure produce in me? Guilt. Anger. Frustration. Rage. So I tried harder. Another failure; more guilt, more anger, more frustration, more rage. After all, wasn't I doing the best I could? Guilt also had company in self-pity ("It's all my fault"). Guilt, anger, frustration, rage, self-pity, and now self-loathing. Nobody likes a failure, especially the one who is failing. What caused all these feelings? *Not knowing I had a choice.*

Today, I know I do. In fact, I have several.

POSSIBLE CHOICES

Following are choices I could have made in the "Reality" scene.

"I fix dinner. He's drunk. I call him to the table. He doesn't move. I eat my dinner and then do something that I've been wanting to do."

"I fix dinner for the whole family. If he isn't ready, the kids and I eat together and talk about what we did today."

"When I see he's out of it, or soon will be, I don't fix dinner at all. The kids and I go out."

"I always leave when he gets like that. Sometimes I take a long walk and just keep repeating, 'Easy does it.' Sometimes I make phone calls I've been putting off."

"I go to my sister's. She has a big family and doesn't mind one more mouth to feed."

What do each of these choices tell us? That the people making them

1. are aware that alcoholism is a disease,
2. are in recovery themselves,
3. know where they are powerless, and
4. know where the power is.

Does it not then follow that if I was powerless over what happened, where it happened, and what made it happen to my husband, that he was powerless over what happened, where it happened, and what made it happen to *me*?

The next discovery: My husband had nothing to do with *my* recovery!

That part felt good. But if he had nothing to do with my recovery, did he have anything to do with my illness? Sure he did! He caused it! Hold on. Did he cause it, or did his disease cause it? *(Pause)* I could blame the chemical, but I couldn't blame my husband anymore. Does it do any good to punish a chemical? No. Does it do any good to blame a chemical? No.

And I finally saw my own insanity. I couldn't carry blame with me anymore.

My husband and I were powerless over each other!

If this is true—and I have only to try otherwise in order to find out that it is—am I not powerless over everybody else? And isn't everybody else powerless over me? Are we not powerless over what happens to others, where it happens, and what makes it happen?

In admitting powerlessness over other people (such as the chemical dependent, the boss who won't see it your way, or the father who has a different political viewpoint), over places (such as, where the car decides to have a flat or where the addict is getting the drugs), and over events (such as, earthquakes and other natural disasters, or the rain that arrives after you've planned a picnic), you will become aware of the power you *do* have. That power comes in the form of choices—not choices over other people, places, and events, but choices that you can make for yourself.

You want control? You've got it. Over *you*.

So being willing to be powerless over everyone but ourselves gives us power over our own choices.

Powerlessness = freedom.

QUESTION

Q. *Why do these choices work better than the screaming you did?*

I've discovered that screaming as a choice doesn't do it for me, because I'll then spend the rest of the evening either justifying my screaming to the user or to myself, or sitting in the guilt I experience when I fly into a rage.

Does that mean I never lose my temper? Of course not. Often, I forget and yell like hell. You can't deny your feelings. You can get to know what they are and learn how to begin to change them, gently.

You've read the "Fantasy" scene on page 12 about the father, mother, and addicted son. Take a look at the following "Reality" scene. Do you see any other choices the father and the mother could have made?

A mother, holding an empty jewelry box, asks her son, "How could you do this?"

Her son is silent.

Her husband says quietly, through his teeth, "Your mother is talking to you."

She begins to cry. "I've raised you to be a good boy. What have I done wrong?"

The father moves in on his son, who's out of it.

"Answer her, damn it!"

He hits his son hard across the face.

"Don't hurt him!"

"He's a junkie! A goddamn, no-good junkie. And the only way to deal with a junkie is to knock it out of him."

He hits his son again.

"Stop it! You're going to kill him."

"I wish to God he was dead! He's no good to anybody."

POSSIBLE CHOICES

"We gave our son an ultimatum: get treatment or get out. He's at a treatment center now. I don't know what tomorrow will bring, but my wife and I are more comfortable today."

"We forced our son into a treatment program, where we're all getting family therapy. My husband and I are now going to Nar-Anon. We're beginning to communicate with our son, but I know that his recovery is ultimately up to him."

"Our son left of his own accord. Neither my wife nor I was able to cut off his funds entirely. After all, he *is* our son, and we feel responsible. We also don't want to take his responsibility away from him, so we reached a compromise. We pay his rent and make sure he has enough food, but we give him no money directly. No choice was easy, but this one seemed the best one for now."

"My wife couldn't take my rage anymore and, frankly, neither could I. I have to first get away from the situation and then decide what I'm going to do after I've cooled down."

"I don't give him money. I do give him love. I can't do anything about his addiction. My husband and I suggest places for him to go, but so far he hasn't tried any of them. Of course it bothers me, but I do sleep at night."

"Our son's been gone for almost two years now. We haven't been able to find him. I pray for him, and life goes on. Of course, I cry. Addiction is a terrible thing. But I don't blame myself anymore."

QUESTION

Q. *I feel like the mother in that scene. I can appreciate the different choices, but will I ever stop worrying?*

It won't happen overnight. But knowing that you are powerless and knowing you have other choices can help you.

If you find yourself stuck on worrying even though you know there is nothing you can do, try taking some kind of action. Work in the garden, go to a movie, call a friend, take a class, help somebody who wants your help. The important thing is to *do* something for yourself.

You may not want to at first. You may want to do nothing but worry, but if you can force yourself to get out of your obsession by taking action, feelings other than worry may soon follow. I'm not saying it's easy, or that it won't come back, or that you can learn to do it overnight. But once you begin to experience more peaceful choices, you'll probably agree that it's worth the effort.

It gets easier to let go of the worry once you get used to substituting something else for it. Just try not to substitute another worry!

You've already read the Lovey/Dovey "Fantasy" scene on page 12. Now, read the Lovey/Dovey "Reality" scene below.

A Sunday morning. Lovey, a young man, and Dovey, a young woman, lie in bed. Her back is to him. He is staring at the ceiling.

"Some party."

There's no response from Dovey.

"Why the hell do you act that way?"

Roughly, he turns her over to face him. "Answer me, goddammit!"

Dovey is hung over, but she speaks with grandiosity. "I do not like to be awakened in such a manner."

"Well, answer me when I'm talking to you!"

"You do not talk. You yell."

He takes her by the shoulders: "You made a fool of yourself!" He imitates her: " 'Mrs. Henlein, you are the picture of my mother.' The woman is younger than you are, for God's sake! 'Mrs. Henlein, you look exactly like my mother!' Over and over again. Before dinner, during dinner, and after."

"Oh, stop exaggerating." She rolls over.

Lovey shakes her roughly. "Don't you *dare* turn your back on me! You made a fool out of *both* of us. I kept changing the subject, and you kept hanging on."

"Leave me alone! I don't even know what you're talking about! You're making me sick!"

She breaks loose and runs into the bathroom, locking the door behind her. We hear her throwing up as Lovey pounds on the door.

EXERCISE

Before you look at the following "Possible Choices," take your notebook and list the choices you might make if *you* were Lovey. List at least three choices—more, if you can.

Whatever your choices, they're great, because you saw that you had them. Unless, of course, you chose to kill Dovey—that's cheating!

Now look at the "Possible Choices" that follow.

POSSIBLE CHOICES

Some choices Lovey could have made:

"I get up before she does in the morning and go for a walk. When I come home, I try not to give her the silent treatment. I figure she feels guilty enough, not because she remembers what she did, but because she doesn't. We get along okay between parties."

"I've had it with Dovey. I choose to live alone."

"I'm not going to parties with her right now. Tomorrow, who knows?"

"I call a buddy and let my anger out about her to him. That usually calms me down, and it doesn't bother him at all."

"We go our own ways at a party. I discovered I can have a good time if I pay attention to me, not her. The next morning? I let her live with her own feelings. If she asks me what she did, I can honestly say I don't know."

"I never bring it up the next morning. She always does, and I tell her what happened if she really wants to know. But I try not to tell her in a punishing way."

"I choose to tell Dovey that if she does it again, we're kaput. Only this time I mean it."

What do all the choices in this chapter have in common? They get our eyes off our obsession with the alcoholic/addict. How do they do that? They are conscious choices of detachment.

QUESTION

Q. *Before those people in the scenes knew they had choices, it was easy to see their obsession with their alcoholics/addicts. But I'm having a hard time seeing mine with my daughter. She doesn't live with us, so most of our contact is by phone. But I worry about her all the time. What can I do?*

If you spend time worrying about her, if you argue

with her on the phone, if you check up on her when she does come home at holidays, if you are angry with her or feel responsible for her habit or believe her when she promises she is clean and you know she isn't, if you think up new ways to try and fix her or repeat old ways that didn't work, if you make excuses for her, if you keep your concern to yourself and brood about it but refuse to share it with your wife because you don't want to worry her, you are obsessed with her.

If her disease is progressive, then maybe yours is, just like my husband's and mine. If you notice your eyes beginning to follow her every move, you may be getting what I call the Mona Lisa syndrome (since da Vinci's sitter seems to watch every move of the viewer). Are you turning into a me? You can choose not to.

You can make a choice like the choices you've been reading about. You can detach from your daughter, detach not with resentment or self-righteousness or self-pity, but with love. And that's our next tool.

8

Getting Off the Stage and into the Audience
Letting Go of the Drama

Do you see anything that the "Reality" scenes you have read have in common with one another? The people and the situations are different, but *all of the scenes are full of drama.* The emotions of the people in each scene are full-blown, either outwardly or inwardly, because the conflict that causes the drama is so enormous.

You may be thinking, "Of course they're full of drama! These are matters of life and death!" And you're right. The problem is that drama doesn't solve anything. In fact, it often creates more problems. And now you may be thinking, "But how can the people in these scenes help it? The feelings they're loaded with are only natural!" And, again, you're right. Rage, self-pity, fear, and whatever else is in these scenes are natural responses to such agonizing situations, but—and this is a big but—they are *not* inevitable. They do *not* have to come up every time one of these scenes occurs.

How can they be prevented? By stifling what you feel? Not at all. By *changing* what you feel? Exactly.

But how can you possibly do that? By remembering the tools you already have in your tool kit: The addict has a disease, you are powerless over the addict and all others, you have power over yourself, and that power allows you to make healthy choices for yourself. All of these tools help you to let go of the drama in your life. The tool we're about to learn now can help you even more.

What is "detaching with love"? Is it some cold, heartless method of ignoring the addict and the problem? No. Is it a choice to leave your environment? Not necessarily. Is it a way to unfasten, unhook, untie yourself from another human being over whom you have no power in a sane, rational, and loving fashion, which will bring you inner peace and help you to get off the back of the addict (an uncomfortable, unsatisfying, and painful place to be in the first place)? Absolutely. But how do you learn to do that?

Perhaps the best way to see what detachment is and how it works is, once again, through example.

Remember the "Fantasy" on page 11 with the addicted mother and the graduating daughter? Take a look at the following "Reality" of the same situation.

A June morning. A daughter, seventeen, who is graduating from high school today, is at the bathroom door. She sees her mother at the medicine chest with a bottle of pills.

"Dad's waiting in the car."

"Be right there," her mother says, as she takes another pill and sways a little.

"Mom, you promised!"

"I'm fine."

"You're stoned!"

"I'm fine." She reaches, unsteadily, for her dress. "Let's go."

"No! I don't want you there! All the kids'll laugh at me!"

The father appears and sees his wife's condition. "Get dressed, dear."

The daughter protests. "No! I don't want her at my graduation! Please, Dad, just you. Not her."

The father helps his wife put the dress over her head. "Your mother should *be* there."

"I'm ashamed of her!"

"Don't talk about your mother that way!"

"You always stick up for her!"

"She'll be fine."

"She'll be asleep!"

He brushes his wife's hair and puts her lipstick on for her. "You look beautiful. Let's go."

"No!" shouts the daughter. "If you bring her, I won't be there!"

"Then you'll go to your graduation alone!"

He gives his daughter the car keys. The daughter runs out the door, in tears.

"I hate you! I hate you both, and I'll never forgive you!!"

This scene is a fine example of the drama we're talking about. What would it be like if both the daughter and the father were able to "detach with love"?

A June morning. A daughter, seventeen, who is graduating from high school today, is at the bathroom door. She sees her mother at the medicine chest with a bottle of pills.

"Time to go, Mom."

Her mother takes another pill and sways a little.

"We're leaving in five minutes. Dad and I will be waiting in the car."

Ten minutes later, the mother still hasn't appeared. The father asks his daughter, "Do you want your mother there?"

"I don't, Daddy. I'm afraid she'll be embarrassing."

"Well, you only graduate from high school once. I want it to be a good one."

The two of them go to the graduation together.

Or:

As the mother comes out of the house, walking shakily, the father asks the daughter, "Do you want your mother there?"

"Yeah. I think I'd feel worse if we drove off without her."

"Okay."

"If she starts a scene, will you take her home?"

"Of course."

He kisses his daughter, then goes to his wife and helps her into the car.

Neither one of these solutions is ideal, right? What we all want is a "happy ending." But since we now know that we can't fix somebody else, these solutions are a heck of a lot better than the intense drama in the "Reality" scene that leaves all three family members devastated.

Both of the above choices made by the father and daughter are choices of detachment from the addict, not with rage or resentment, but with love.

Let's experience the tools one more time. Both the father and the daughter are aware that the mother has a disease. Thus the compassion. They also know that they are powerless to make her well. Thus the acceptance. Knowing that they have the power to make the choice that will help themselves, they make the choice of detachment with love in both examples, because it seems to be the best choice to make. Detaching from the problem (that is, the mother's addiction) lets them stay in the solution. They then take positive action. The father supports the daughter. The daughter chooses to go either with her mother or without her mother, whichever is more comfortable for her. Both the father and daughter love the mother but not her addiction, and they let her know this through their actions, without the drama.

The father and the daughter thus "got off the stage and into the audience." They stood back and looked at the situation. They refused to participate in the old scene. They made new choices that helped them face the problem and decide what to do about it. They detached from the mother, with love, and continued with their important day, which they were able to share together.

The solution is no dream come true? You bet it isn't. But it's the best there was in such a trying and traumatic situation. Chemical dependency is cunning, baffling, and insidious.

Why is detaching with love so hard to do? For me, it was almost impossible in the beginning to stand back far enough to detach at all. I would consciously choose to do it, yet I couldn't. I had to be very patient with myself. Patience is very important in using every tool. Have it with yourself.

Again, the more you're willing to try a new tool, the easier it becomes.

QUESTIONS

Q. *I want to detach with love from my addicted sister, but when she's around I'm too filled with rage to be able to do it. How can I change that?*

There are times when detaching physically from the person is the best you can do, since you cannot deny your feelings. Try making the choice to leave the house when your sister is high, and don't forget to take your rage with you. In the car, instead of justifying your rage, let it out. Go ahead and scream. If you're not in a car, go to a friend's, and let it out there.

Once the rage begins to subside, you can feel better about one thing. You didn't let your sister have it, so you won't have the guilt to contend with. You can feel better about another thing, too. You started the process of detaching. You made a choice that you saw yourself making. You have begun to stand back and look at *you*. Miracle of miracles, you weren't looking at *her*. Another step on the road to recovery—your own.

Q. *I love my wife. Isn't it cruel to leave her alone when she gets drunk?*

She's not alone. She has her chemical. But nobody says you have to walk out on her. You can go to another room. The point is not to sit there and try to reason with a chemical or to punish your wife with your disapproval. It helps some people to think of detaching from the problem, not from the person. Then you are free to continue to love the person but not the chemical. It's more cruel to yourself to stay, mentally or physically. You can do nothing for her.

Q. *I hate my dad. When he is using, he yells at me and won't let me leave. I'm only thirteen. What can I do?*

If he allows you to leave the room, do it. Call a friend and talk about the feelings running through you.

If he makes you stand there and take it, you can choose to let go of what you're hearing. Imagine he's talking in Chinese: then his words can't hurt you. Or look at him for what he is: ill.

And if you want to, you can talk to him the next day, if he's clean. If he doesn't remember what he said, you can tell him and then let it go. You can let him know that when he gets like that he hurts your feelings. You can tell him you love him but not what he does.

Choosing to do it privately, when he's sober, is detaching with love, too.

Perhaps the most helpful choice would be to try Alateen. There are kids there in the same boat as you are.

Q. *My wife is so helpless when she's high. Can't I help her?*

Nobody says you should not help her. The question is, what *does* help her?

Don't do for your wife what she has to do for herself. We can't carry a toddler around all the time because we don't want him to fall. He'll never learn to walk, and certainly he'll resent us for that.

What *can* you do? You can love her, and proceed with your own tasks. Getting you healthy *is* your responsibility.

You are powerless over her, remember? Can you work on emotionally detaching? It's so much better for both of you. If you have the right to choose for yourself, doesn't she?

(I can feel you heading for another tunnel now, thinking: "Yes, but *she's* too sick to do it. *I* have to." That's called "playing God.")

Q. *My husband will get fired if I don't lie to his boss. How will we live?*

You're filled with fear of the future. That's understandable. When I get like that, I have to remind myself to live one day at a time, because that's all I have.

You cannot save your husband. He has a progressive disease. By lying to his boss, you may be prolonging the agony.

Detaching with love allows you to make choices for yourself, choices you may not have thought about for a long time. Ask yourself some questions: What do I want to do at this moment? What will give me pleasure? What will make me feel better? You may not know the answers anymore, but keep asking. The answers will come.

Does that sound selfish? It did to me. But I'm learning that that kind of selfishness is healthy. It permits me to enjoy myself. As I'm more able to make these choices, I'm more able to love me. And as I'm more able to love me, I'm more able to love another person freely, without obsession. And that's detaching with love.

I know it's hard, but you can do it. Get into the audience, preferably the second balcony, and watch the star of the show—you.

The funny thing about watching yourself is that it frees you *from* yourself.

REVIEW

In accepting that alcoholism/addiction is a disease, we discovered that we, too, are emotionally diseased. We need help. A big help is to see that we are powerless not only over the addict but over everyone else as well. Once we begin to learn that, we are able to see that we have choices for ourselves that give us power over our own lives.

Seeing that we have choices is one thing; being able to make them is another. Once we understand the meaning of detaching with love, we can more easily begin to make conscious choices that will be healthier for us.

At this point you may be asking, "Doesn't she realize she's told us this over and over?" Yes, she does. But she didn't get it the first time. Once she did begin to get it, she'd forget it. She has also discovered that repeating what she is getting over and over takes what she is getting to a deeper level each time. Why do you think she keeps going to meetings?

Once is not enough.

9

Chain Reactions

Letting Go of Having to Be Perfect

All of the tools we've learned about so far can help us to stand back and take a look at ourselves. Each tool makes the focus a little clearer. The tool we're about to deal with gave me an even sharper picture. I didn't like what I saw, so in the beginning I chose not to see it.

How could I avoid looking at myself? By justifying why I did what I did, pinning the blame on somebody else. At least, *I* was always right. Forget the fact that living that way didn't work.

My sponsor had me look at my "Reality" scene (page 14) once more.

SPONSOR: What filled you with rage in that scene?

ME: My husband.

SPONSOR: How?

ME: He wouldn't come to dinner.

SPONSOR: So, your husband's not coming to dinner filled you with rage.

ME: Yes.

SPONSOR: If your husband hadn't been drinking, would he have come to dinner?

ME: Yes, I guess so.

SPONSOR: So it wasn't really your husband who filled you with rage. It was his drinking.

ME: Right.

SPONSOR: What was your husband doing to you by drinking?

ME: He made me ruin my meat loaf.

SPONSOR: So your rage was caused by a ruined meat loaf.

ME: Yes. Which he made me ruin.

SPONSOR: Were you aware that the meat loaf had been cooked enough?

ME: I don't know.

SPONSOR: Had you ever cooked a meat loaf before?

ME: Yes, but—(*Here we go with the game again.*)

SPONSOR: Then you knew how long a meat loaf takes to cook.

ME: Yes, but—

SPONSOR: So, you could have taken it out when it was cooked, and not been in a rage?

ME: Yes, but—

SPONSOR: Do you know why you didn't?

ME: Because I wanted him to come to dinner and eat the meat loaf with me!

SPONSOR: And would he?

ME: No!

SPONSOR: When I get into a rage, it's usually my will that sends me there. Was it your will that he wasn't obeying?

ME: Yes. He was obeying his own.

SPONSOR: And what did that do to you?

ME: It made me fly into a rage!

SPONSOR: So when your will is not obeyed, you react by flying into a rage.

ME: I couldn't help it. He *made* me go into one!

SPONSOR: Rage was not your choice of action?

ME: No!

SPONSOR: What was it then?

ME: My *re*action!

SPONSOR: (*very gently*) So, by not knowing that you were powerless, by not knowing you had a choice to act differently, by being unable to detach from your husband, you simply reacted to what your husband did or didn't do.

ME: Yes.

SPONSOR: Do you want to learn how to change your reactions?

ME: No! I was right! He was wrong!

SPONSOR: But you're still carrying the incident with you by blaming him for it. Wouldn't you like to erase the blackboard?

ME: Not with the meat-loaf incident! I was right!

SPONSOR: Can you think of another incident that filled you with rage besides the meat-loaf incident?

ME: Hundreds.

SPONSOR: Go home and write.

ME: About what?

SPONSOR: About incidents from your past that you're still justifying.

ME: I'm still justifying them because I'm still right!

SPONSOR: Does hanging on to being right further your own recovery?

ME: Well, I'm *not* going to write about the meat-loaf incident. That one I *was* right about.

SPONSOR: Fine.

ME: And the ones that come to mind have nothing to do with my husband.

SPONSOR: Good. Write about the ones that have to do with others.

ME: Why?

SPONSOR: It'll help you to see that the tools are not just for helping you in your relationship with your husband. They'll help you in your relationships with everybody. Your rage didn't start with your husband, did it?

ME: I'm sure I had a little before I met him. He wasn't the *only* thing wrong in my life.

SPONSOR: Write about a few of the others. Simply describe what happened and see what comes up for you.

I wrote about the woman who stepped in front of me at the checkout line, and I wrote about my dog who peed on the carpet, and I wrote about the guy I'd hired whom I overheard telling somebody else I wasn't any good at my job. I did a lot of writing, and do you know what came up for me? Justification after justification after justification. And who stayed unhappy for the rest of the day, continuing to find more justifications? Me.

Then came a revelation. What's so great about having to be

right when being right feels miserable? When I stopped justify-ing my "rightness," I was forced to answer, "Not a damn thing."

I did *not* want to let in what I'd just discovered. Not only my rage but also my guilt and my self-pity, my entire bundle of emotions, were caused by my own reactions.

When I was little, I had an excuse. I was little. I didn't know any better. But I wasn't little when the dog peed on the carpet. Nevertheless, I still didn't know any better. My reaction was to fly into a rage.

And who was hurt by the rage?

Not the dog. He knew what to do. He detached with love immediately.

Not the kids. They don't even remember the incident.

The one hurt by the rage was the one consumed by the rage.

When I calmed down, where did the rage go? It went deep inside me and turned into guilt, because I had screamed at the dog and the kids. And there it got stuck until I found another tool in the program, which I'll share later. Now I can laugh about it—from the second balcony. But I couldn't then.

I went back to my sponsor and told her what I'd discovered.

"But I can't change my reactions!" I said to her over and over.

"Try substituting the word *won't* for *can't*. If that makes you angry, that's your reaction. But if you are willing to give it a try, you can begin by taking one little reaction at a time. You won't always succeed, but the more you do it, the easier it will be-come, just like every other tool."

At last, I was able to go back to the meat loaf.

It was my reaction to the meat loaf that screwed me up. I could have taken it out earlier, or laughed when I did take it out. It was pretty funny-looking.

It was my reaction to my husband's drinking that screwed me up. Had I been able to look at him as diseased, I could have had another reaction—one that wouldn't have filled me with rage, one that wouldn't have made such a terrible memory, one that wouldn't have lingered so long.

It was my reaction to his drinking, to his yelling, to a look on his face, or to a change in his tone of voice. It was *my reaction.*

And it wasn't just my reactions to people that got me into trouble. If I was here and I wanted to be there, my frustration ruined what was going on here. If I was stuck in traffic and was forced to be late for something, my anxiety destroyed my serenity.

I created the battlefields in my life. In order to get off them, all I had to do was stop justifying why I pulled my trigger. In other words, I had to let go of having to be right. What's the big deal about being right, anyway?

I don't have to be perfect anymore. Neither does anybody else. Not today, anyway.

QUESTIONS

Q. *My daughter is hooked on cocaine! How the hell can you say that it is my reaction to her addiction that causes the trouble?*

Your reaction to her addiction does not cause your daughter's trouble. It causes your own. As much as you would like to solve your daughter's problem, you can't. I keep harking back to powerlessness, because it's when I forget that I am powerless over someone else that I find myself in trouble again.

Suppose that your daughter calls you. She's been kicked out of her apartment and wants to move back in with you and your wife. You are furious with her (your reaction to her problem is rage), but you are afraid of what will happen if you don't put a roof over her head, so you let her move back in. Your life becomes a nightmare because she won't listen to you. She will not obey your will. She's full of her own. She plays her music too loud. She brings guys home. She borrows money from you and doesn't pay you back. She's messy. She gets sick. You have to take care of her. Her dealer comes to the house. And on and on and on.

The concept that it is your reactions to your daughter that fill you with misery still stands. She runs you.

She has enormous power over you, because you are obsessed with what she does or does not do. The anger, the rage, the guilt, and the self-pity are your reactions to her. Nobody can *make* you feel these things. Nobody except you.

Q. *But I have to react with anger. How else will she know that I disapprove of what she's doing?*

If anger is your choice for letting her know that you disapprove of her, go ahead and choose it. But aren't you forgetting that your daughter has a disease?

Try substituting the word *diabetes* for *addiction,* and listen to how that sounds:

"Stop having that diabetes!" (*Anger*)

"If you'll stop being diabetic, I'll pay your car insurance." (*Bribery*)

"Please, I beg of you. Don't have diabetes anymore." (*Begging*)

"If you don't stop being diabetic, you can get out!" (*Threat*)

"Can't you see what you're doing to me and your mother by refusing to stop being diabetic?" (*Guilt producing*)

We who love alcoholics/addicts use all of these ploys until we are willing to believe that addiction is a disease.

I don't think any of us can hear these words too often: We did not cause the addiction, we can't control the addiction, and we can't cure it. The addict's addiction can be arrested if the addict seeks help in a support group or treatment center, but only if the addict is willing to let the help in. Sometimes the addict is able to arrest his or her own disease without outside help. But even then, we—the relatives and friends—do not arrest it for him or her.

Q. *Then what can I do?*

Exactly what you're doing now. You can be working on your own recovery. Taking your eyes off your daughter gives you time to look at you. You are free to change as much as you like. Every new attitude you choose contributes to a new way of life.

You can have a better relationship with your daughter, if you so choose—even a better relationship than you've ever had. Perhaps as equals. Perhaps as friends. All you have to do is accept her, let go of her with love, and let her know how you feel.

If you are confused about your feelings, tell her that. Listen to what she has to say, if she wants to talk. Keep the lines of communication open.

Just as you are coming to believe that you are powerless over her, let yourself believe that *she is powerless over you.* Then there is nothing left except love. Let her know that.

Once you have allowed yourself to be soft and warm and vulnerable with her, *do not* expect her to behave differently as a result of your opening up. You have no control over the outcome. That is not the motive for connecting with her. The motive is to feel more at peace with yourself, and your honesty will allow you to do just that, because you know you can do no more.

Think about what you want to do the next time you see her. Get off the stage and into the audience, and create the scene. You can't put words into her mouth. You can't give her her lines. You can't write her script, but you *can* write your own.

If you didn't love her, you wouldn't feel so strongly about her in the first place. The next time you see her, look at her and remind yourself to accept her, to forgive her, to think of the love you feel for her.

Q. *Will I ever be able to trust her again?*

Oh, my friend, my heart goes out to you. Your question is the same question *I* had for so long. I've never met a relative or friend who didn't have it.

I have never found the definitive answer. I think that the wide-eyed, innocent kind of trust is gone, and I doubt it will ever come back. At least, it hasn't in my experience. That kind of trust is like the experience of being in love for the first time. It's never the same again. But that doesn't mean it can't be just as good, and in many ways, even better.

I feel it's time for a break.

You've already gotten off the stage. Why not get out of the audience and take an intermission? Treat yourself. Soak in the tub. Take some slow, deep breaths. Listen to music you love. Hug somebody. Hug yourself. Do something that will bring you some peace.

If I were my old controlling self, I would suggest that you go to a meeting, because that's where *I* find peace. But I know that I am powerless over what you do—I know that *at this moment*—so I choose to back off and let you choose.

The question of trust is such a universal one that it deserves a chapter to itself. When you come back, we'll give it one.

10

You Can't Go Home Again

Letting Go of Having to Trust

The universal question is this: When will I be able to trust the addict again?

The answers you want to hear are the following:

A. When he tells you he has stopped using.
B. When you are given the key to make him stop using.
C. When he stops using.

How about A? "When he tells you he has stopped using."?

Sounds good, but has he ever *admitted* using? If so, has he ever told you before that he has stopped using? Can you believe him this time? If he hasn't ever told you this before, can you believe that he is telling you the truth?

No, A doesn't seem to be it.

Then there's B: "When you are given the key to make him stop using."

If you find the key, I hope you are willing to share it. I looked for it for half my life, and I never found it. If you can look at addiction as a disease similar in nature to diabetes, I think you will be willing to discard B. At least for today.

Finally, C: "When he stops using."

C is probably the most popular choice. But even if you believe it, doesn't it lead to another question? And that question is this: But what if he starts using again? When you get to this question, do you not have to go back to A, B, or C again?

The interesting thing is that people who have been in the program for a while seldom ask the universal question about trust. I don't. I know I will never trust my husband's disease, and he will never be cured. But I believe I'll always trust my husband, whether he drinks again or not. His disease is not him. And I trust that if he drinks again, he will find his own way back, with the help of his program. But I won't *expect* him to. Expectations get me into trouble.

I honestly think that trust plays a less and less important role in a relationship the more you come to accept the other person.

If the user is a child, you'll never be able to go back to what the two of you had together when she was a *child* child, but you can't have that with *any* adult child anyway, can you? (That's one of the reasons that relationships with grandchildren are so great!)

The innocence that disappears does not have to be replaced with something bad. It *can* be replaced with something better— a closeness you've never shared before, because you've been through so much together. All it requires is acceptance on your part. Is it possible for you to let go of the distrust and replace it with acceptance? Are you willing to try it? Not once, but as many times as necessary until you can experience what acceptance feels like?

11

Name It, Claim It
Letting Go of the Secret Demons

If one of the purposes of these tools is to be able to keep our eyes on ourselves and off others, we have to be willing to be honest with ourselves and accept what we see. Only then can we begin to change those parts of us that are making us ill, that are preventing our own growth, our own recovery. Difficult as the process may be, I found it invaluable. After a while it almost got to be fun, but only after I became willing to look at, and take responsibility for, my "secret demons." Why did I keep them a secret for so long? Because I thought I was the only one who was possessed.

This is going to be a long chapter. How can you rush through demons that took a lifetime to collect?

As my husband's disease of alcoholism progressed, so too did my disease of being obsessed with his disease, although I was unaware that either of us had a disease. "I knew what was best" for him. When he didn't listen, I became angry with him and sorry for myself, because I was only doing this "for his own good."

How could I possibly take my eyes off him? Without me, he would be "lost." In order to "save him," I *had* to keep my eyes on his every move, so I could tell him what to do or not to do. This is known in the program as "taking someone's inventory."

I'd had experience doing inventory work before I met my husband, and living with an alcoholic for so long had made me one of the top inventory-takers in the country.

So I took my family's inventories, my friends' inventories, and strangers' inventories. I gave advice to all, even though no one ever took it. They were a disappointing bunch. But surely someone, somewhere would be wise enough to listen to me, and the world would be a better place. So I kept on trying to change others.

Then my sponsor said that since I had become such an expert at taking others' inventories, perhaps it was time to put my expertise to better use. She suggested that I take my own inventory. What was she talking about?

I asked her *why* I should do this. She said self-examination leads to self-recovery, and the examination of another doesn't.

I bought more paper for my three-ring notebook. As it turned out, a *lot* more paper.

It was not easy to start digging into old hurts, old wounds, things I had kept hidden for so long. Of course, I hadn't forgotten them, no matter how hard I'd tried. They sat there, defying me to come and get them. And as I remembered them, it was as though I was reliving them all over again.

More than once, I felt overwhelmed by the task. There was so much to cover. So much, in fact, that I was forced to take my eyes off others. Believe me, I wasn't sure they would be able to get along without me, but they managed somehow. After the shock of discovering that they didn't need me to take their inventories, I began to enjoy my own.

Why did I put myself through a self-inventory? I noticed that those who had already done it seemed to have a self-acceptance and an honesty about themselves that I had never been able to experience. In other words, I wanted what they had, once again, and the only way I knew to get it was to do what they did.

Why did I wait so long? I was deathly afraid of what I might find because I wanted so much to think I was perfect. I figured that if I ignored those little demons inside me long enough, they would quietly disappear. But they never did. I *had* to look at myself.

I hadn't ever done that before. I had spent all my time looking at others.

I didn't know where to begin.

My sponsor suggested that I take one incident at a time (this had never occurred to me) and that I start with one from the past that seemed like nothing, except that the tape was continuing to play somewhere in my head.

Before I begin the self-inventory, let me say that I'm very aware that the childhood theft I'm going to tell about must seem like nothing to those of you who are suffering a life-and-death trauma at this very moment because there is a substance abuser in your life who is destroying himself or herself. But I am very grateful that my sponsor asked me to begin with what I thought was a trivial inventory. It made it easier to tackle the really big ones later on. If you decide to take this tool and use it, you may want to start out in a similar manner. Remember, easy does it.

The following is an example of the beginning of an inventory. This particular method is the one my sponsor used, so that's what she recommended for me. There are many, many different methods for doing a self-inventory, one as valuable as another. Another sponsor might have shown me another method. There is no one right way.

A SELF-INVENTORY ON A CHILDHOOD THEFT

The Incident

When I was about thirteen, I worked in a tiny ice-cream store called DeVito's.

I had a manager, Mrs. Eckles. She was tight. She never let me have one taste of ice cream, which was my favorite food in the world. Since I only made twenty-five cents an hour, I felt justified in pigging out on the black raspberry ice cream when she left the store for a few minutes one night. I got a spoon and dug in.

By the time she returned, I had stuffed down at least a quart. She looked in the cash register and asked, "How was business?"

"Not too good," I answered.

She peered into the containers. "My, we had a run on black raspberry." She kept staring at me. "You look green. Are you all right?"

"I'm fine," I lied.

"Look," she said. "Why don't you go home? We're not busy."

I stumbled out of the store and threw up all the way home.

To begin, I listed my feelings.

My Feelings

1. I felt justified in stealing the ice cream. She had given me no choice.
2. I resented her stinginess, and I wanted to get back at her. She was a mean old lady.
3. She shouldn't have treated me like that. I worked hard for twenty-five cents an hour!
4. I was scared to death she'd fire me if she found out.
5. I was too ashamed to tell her I *was* feeling sick.
6. I felt guilty then because I knew stealing was wrong, and even though I spent years "being right," I still feel guilty today.

After I had written the story and listed my feelings, my sponsor asked me to read them to her.

"Read them to you? Out loud? Are you nuts?"

But I did read them to her, and she didn't think I was rotten at all. She told me of a similar incident from *her* past.

Next, she suggested that I look for any defects in what I had read to her.

ME: Sure. Mrs. Eckles was tight and didn't appreciate me, and that's why I acted the way I did.

SPONSOR: Can you change Mrs. Eckles?

ME: No. She's dead.

She smiled, but she wouldn't let me off the hook.

SPONSOR: Could you have changed her then?

ME: I sure wanted to.

SPONSOR: But could you?

ME: *No, but* I didn't know that then.

SPONSOR: Do you know it now?

ME: *Yes, but—*

SPONSOR: What *can* you change?

ME: I don't think I can change anything. It already happened.

SPONSOR: Can you change the way you view it today?

ME: I don't know.

SPONSOR: Are you willing to try?

ME: *Yes, but—*

SPONSOR: Good. Now, let's look for the defects.

ME: I already told you the defects. She was tight, and she didn't appreciate—

SPONSOR: Not *her* defects. *Yours.*

ME: *My* defects? She *made* me do what I did!

SPONSOR: How?

ME: She never offered me any ice cream!

SPONSOR: So the only way to get it was to steal it.

ME: Exactly.

SPONSOR: Okay. And in whom has the incident been lodged all these years? Mrs. Eckles?

ME: No. Me.

SPONSOR: Can you change Mrs. Eckles, dead *or* alive?

Her patience drove me crazy.

ME: No!

SPONSOR: Who caused the demons in the first place?

ME: Mrs. Eckles!

SPONSOR: Did you ever ask her for some ice cream?

ME: No. She would have said no.

SPONSOR: Or she might have said yes.

ME: You didn't know Mrs. Eckles!

SPONSOR: You're right. But could you have asked her?

ME: No!

SPONSOR: Why not?

ME: It would have been futile!

SPONSOR: So therefore you couldn't ask her.
ME: I *wouldn't* ask her.
SPONSOR: Why?
ME: Because I was afraid of her!
SPONSOR: Whose *demon* is that?

And the walls came a-tumbling down.

Mrs. Eckles didn't do anything to me. It didn't matter whether she would have given me ice cream or not. It was my own fear that drove me to steal the ice cream in the first place. My own fear plus several other defects, all belonging to me, and all of them reactions (there's that word again) to Mrs. Eckles's not doing what I wanted her to do. I wanted her to change, and she was not about to, not unless she *chose* to change. Mrs. Eckles was just like my husband—and everybody else.

I was now willing to list my character defects, but I hated the word *defects*.

ME: Can't I call them something else?
SPONSOR: Sure.
ME: How about *faults*?
SPONSOR: Do you like that better?
ME: No. *Faults* make me feel like I did bad things. How about *goofs*?
SPONSOR: Fine.
ME: No. Not important enough. *Sins*? God, no. Okay, *defects*. But I don't want to read them to you.
SPONSOR: Why not?
ME: You'll see how imperfect I am.
SPONSOR: Can you let go of having to be perfect?
ME: Yeah, I can let go of *me* having to think I am, but I still want *you* to think I am.
SPONSOR: If I can love me, warts and all, I can love you, warts and all.
ME: You don't know my warts.
SPONSOR: Sure I do. They're the same as mine.

I went home and sat down to list my defects in the raspberry ice-cream incident.

But there was a problem. Hard as I looked, I couldn't find them. I didn't want to see my own defects. All these years I knew I must have done some "bad" things in my life because I had a lot of guilt, but I never wanted to know about the part I had played in what had happened to me.

My sponsor helped me. It was hard at first. It got easier. All it required was that I be willing to see them (that is, name them) and accept them as mine. In other words, be willing to take responsibility for them—not blame, but responsibility (claim them).

Why is it important to give them a name and accept them as my responsibility? Because I am better able to look at them, there, on a piece of paper, to stand back further, to stop blaming others and myself, to be an observer instead of a judge. Instead of feeling how "bad" I am or how "bad" others have been to me, I am better able to see how human we all are.

How about the word *shortcomings*? Is that any better? Same thing.

My Defects:

1. *Dishonesty*: I stole the ice cream.
2. *Greed*: I made myself sick.
3. *Blame*: She made me do it.
4. *Pride*: I was ashamed to tell Mrs. Eckles.
5. *Self-justification*: If she hadn't been so stingy, I wouldn't have had to steal it.
6. *Anger/Resentment*: She never gave me any ice cream.
7. *Judgment*: She was a stingy old lady.
8. *Revenge*: I'll show her.
9. *Fear*: Of being caught.
10. *Guilt*: Stealing is wrong.
11. *Lack of self-esteem*: I was a bad girl.

SPONSOR: Do you see anything else?
ME: Nope.
SPONSOR: No self-pity?

The moment she said this, another wall came a-tumbling down. I felt really good about seeing that one. There was a relief in getting it out on paper!

12. *Self-pity*: I work so hard, and where does it get me?

SPONSOR: That's it?
ME: I can't see any more.
SPONSOR: Who was wrong in this?
ME: *She* was.

13. *Self-righteousness:* I looked at the list of feelings and the list of defects. And I called this a "nothing"?

Funny. After looking at all the defects I was filled with, I had no trouble with the concept of a *"lower* power." How come I was having trouble with the concept of a *higher* one?

QUESTIONS

Q. *What I want to know is, does a bad memory go away once you do an inventory?*

Not for me. I can't change what happened, but I can change the way I look at it. I can see the mountain I made out of a molehill. As soon as I can let go of blaming Mrs. Eckles, all I can see is the molehill, and I feel more and more at peace. As a matter of fact, today, as I remember the incident, I see an anthill. Who knows? Maybe in time there will be nothing left but an empty hole in which I can store a good memory.

Q. *If it's my reactions that get me into trouble, does this mean that I am to blame for all the unhappiness in my life?*

Great question. That's exactly how I felt when I started taking my own inventory: "You mean, if Mrs. Eckles didn't do anything to me, then I'm the one at fault? That feels worse than blaming Mrs. Eckles!"

What I began to see is that there is no blame. What is blame? Blame is judgment, of oneself or of somebody else. What am I doing when I judge myself or another? I am playing God. Am I God? Of course not. Then who am I to sit back and do the judging? I have to keep reminding myself: I am not God. I am not God. I am not God. I'm human. Humans have defects. Past defects become deep dark secrets, secrets we keep not only from others but also from ourselves. We're *afraid* to look at them, *afraid* to take responsibility for them. But fear only gives them more power.

What takes their power away? Being willing to let go of them by taking honest stock of yourself and taking your own inventory, so that you can see the part you played in the events of your life.

I went to work with great trepidation. The incident contained almost every defect known to humankind. What was I letting myself in for? To this day, I can't look at black raspberry ice cream even *after* doing an inventory. My sponsor suggested I turn that into a "grateful."

Me: Why?
Sponsor: Look at the calories you've saved!

Her cup is always half full.

EXERCISE

Before continuing, try doing a sample inventory on one of your own childhood incidents. In your notebook, write the story, list your feelings (both then and now), and pick out your defects. Don't keep any secrets, and don't paint a "nicer" picture of yourself. It's not as big a deal as you think.

It's a game. Concentrate on what you're doing so that judgment of yourself doesn't creep in and prevent you from "letting it all hang out."

The following outline may help you.

The Incident

(After you've written it, let yourself relive as much as you can the feelings you had when the incident occurred.)

My Feelings

My Defects

(If you're not sure what your defects are, here's a list of common ones. I've experienced them all. You may have, too.)

Fear

Anger (rage)

Pride (embarrassment/shame)

Envy/Jealousy

Self-pity

Self-righteousness

Self-loathing (lack of self-esteem)

Character assassination

Guilt

Greed

Sloth

Self-will

Judgment

Lack of responsibility

Overly strong sense of responsibility (having to control)

Revenge

Resentment

You may think of others, or you may choose another name for one already on the list. Whatever hits home, put it down. The person with the longest list wins the blue ribbon for honesty. Unless, of course, you are naming and claiming *another's* defects in the incident. Name and claim only *yours*.

ANOTHER SELF-INVENTORY

Once I'd done a few "light" ones, I became willing to tackle a much heavier one.

The Incident

A number of years ago, my husband and I were having dinner with another couple. He proceeded to get drunk and obnoxious with all of us. I was embarrassed. We left the restaurant, and I insisted on driving home. On the way home, I began to yell at him for behaving so abominably. I was relentless. He started pounding me on the head. I stopped the car and jumped out. He chased after me. He caught up with me. I socked him, ran back to the car, jumped in, and began to chase after him in the car, as he headed down the street. I tried to make him get back in the car. He wouldn't. I drove home by myself, justifying my behavior, and worried all night that he would get killed.

I come out smelling like a rose, don't I? After all, didn't he cause the incident? If he hadn't been drunk, it never would have happened, right?

Right. But it did happen, and it attached itself—to me. Didn't it attach itself to him? My guess is it did, but only my husband knows for sure.

Didn't my husband owe me an apology? Of course he did, and he made one the following day. But what if he hadn't apologized? Then he would have to live with that, just as I have to live with the part I played in the whole thing until I make the choice to mind my *own* business by taking my *own* inventory.

I made the choice.

My business is taking a look at the part *I* played that caused me to hurt both of us. I verbally attacked him, not once but over and over. I wanted to take revenge on him for embarrassing me. I wanted to *punish him*. The revenge is my responsibility. Playing God is my responsibility. Neither one of these choices, unconscious though they may have been, worked. I felt guilty afterward.

This incident remained lodged inside me long after he had apologized. My sponsor asked me to list my feelings, just as I'd done for the incident involving Mrs. Eckles.

My Feelings

1. I was filled with rage when he got drunk.
2. I was embarrassed, ashamed of his behavior. I felt it reflected on me.
3. I was afraid he'd hurt himself. I was afraid he'd hurt me.
4. I blamed him for ruining my evening.
5. I felt sorry for myself.
6. My anger was justified. He had started it.
7. I felt "bad" that I had socked him.

My Defects

1. *Rage*: At him.
2. *Pride*: Embarrassment/shame.
3. *Fear*: *Of* him and *for* him.
4. *Resentment*: He had ruined my evening.
5. *Self-pity*: Why me?

6. *Self-justification*: He had started it.
7. *Guilt*: I had provoked him.
8. *Lack of self-esteem*: I felt "bad."
9. *Self-righteousness*: I was right. He was wrong.

QUESTIONS

Q. *Why are you letting the abuser off the hook?*

At the time of the incident, I didn't "let the abuser off the hook." Far from it. I had "let him have it" when he was nothing but a walking bottle. What good had it done me to let him have it? I felt guilty, I held a grudge, and I justified my action for years. That is not letting *myself* off the hook. An honest self-inventory allows me to stop taking responsibility for his actions and to take responsibility for my own.

Q. *How can I give up judging somebody else?*

I don't know if I'll ever stop judging others in a negative way entirely. But I am doing it less now because I see myself doing it, and when I can I try to look at the person I'm judging in a different way. I try to find something I like, or I try to see why I'm judging that particular trait, or I work on being grateful that I am who I am, or I choose to listen and see if there is anything I can learn.

I don't do this for the other person. I do it for me.

It is important to remember that the inventory tool, like all other tools, is to make *you* feel better, to give *you* more peace with yourself and with others, to pave the way for *your own* self-acceptance, and to lead *you* to self-love, which allows you to love others.

Q. *But isn't finding something you like judging another person?*

Sure, but I'm *comfortable* with it.

Q. *But if the addict doesn't do an inventory, why should you?*

It's so easy to forget why we choose to do an inventory. The inventory tool is to help us with our *own* recovery. Keeping our eyes on ourselves, minding our own business, and making choices for ourselves contribute to that recovery.

EXERCISE

You've done an inventory on one of your own childhood incidents. How about acting as if you were the son in the following incident? Try listing his feelings and picking out his defects before you read his own lists of these.

A Son's Inventory: The Incident

My dad called and said he'd lost his job. He was unable to pay his rent and asked me if I'd help him out. I sent him a check. He promised to give it to the landlord the next day. Two weeks later, the landlord called me and said he was going to kick him out because he hadn't paid his rent. I drove over and found my dad so out of it he was incoherent. We had a big blowup. I refused to give him another check. My sister felt sorry for him and paid his rent. I think they're both crazy. Of course, my dad promises he will go straight now, but I know he's lying.

In your notebook, list what you think are the son's feelings, and then list his defects.

Now read his own lists.

My Feelings

1. My dad makes me furious, and no wonder!
2. He embarrasses me.

3. I resent him.
4. What did I do to deserve this?
5. I'm afraid he's killing himself.
6. My sister is wrong to do what she does.
7. I feel like I've failed somehow.
8. I feel he should be punished for what he's doing to himself, and I don't like myself for feeling that.
9. I want him to change.

My Defects

1. *Rage*: At Dad.
2. *Pride*: He makes me look bad.
3. *Resentment*: Toward Dad.
4. *Self-pity*: Why me?
5. *Fear*: He'll die.
6. *Self-justification*: I'm furious *because*—
7. *Anger*: At my sister.
8. *Self-righteousness*: My sister's wrong. I'm right.
9. *Lack of self-esteem*: I've failed.
10. *Guilt*: For wanting to see him punished.
11. *Judgment*: I've failed; my dad's crazy; my sister's crazy.
12. *Revenge*: He should be punished. He's punishing us.
13. *Self-will*: I want him to change!

Your initial response to the son's predicament is likely to be, "He's right, by God!" But an inventory has nothing to do with right or wrong. An inventory has to do with taking a look at yourself and at the part you played in situations that hurt and wounded you.

Inventories are *not* about blame. Naming your defects and then taking responsibility for them is only being willing to admit that you are human. We *all* have defects. We all have the same defects. The proportions may be different, that's all. I didn't know that, so I kept them hidden. I had to be right in a situation or else I would have had to admit my imperfections.

Look again at the son/father situation. Why does the son do an inventory? He wants to feel peace within himself, to experience some sense of well-being. He *can't* make his dad stop using. He is powerless. He *can* take a look at the part he played in this incident and begin to change himself.

If he keeps trying, and failing, to save his dad, he keeps reacting with the same feelings that are screwing him up. Doing this is like butting your head against a stone wall again and again, even though it hurts.

I know it's natural for the son to react as he does. But that's not getting *him* any better, and that's why he's choosing the tool in the first place.

His dad is an addict. What is he doing to his son? Manipulating him? You bet. He'll do anything to get his drug. But no one can manipulate anyone unless that person chooses to be manipulated.

What does the son want the father to do? More than anything else, he wants him to live. Can he control that? No. He isn't his dad's higher power. He is powerless over what his dad does or doesn't do. With that said, can the son try to help the father? Yes, he can try, once he knows what help really is.

Help is letting the addict know that you love him and are there for him. Help is learning about the disease of addiction so that you can better understand the addict. Help is allowing the addict to hit his own bottom, whatever that may be. Help is not taking the addict's responsibility away from him. Help is refusing to be a doormat.

And after you've done everything you know to do, how can you most help the addict? By letting go of him or her, with love, and going to work on your own recovery.

And how can you most help yourself? By letting go of him or her, with love, and going to work on your own recovery.

QUESTIONS

Q. *Do you have to say the same thing over and over and over?*

I think so. Breaking those habits that are the symptoms of our disease is tough work. Repetition is a necessary reminder.

Q. *I understand the value of self-inventory. But do I actually have to read my inventory to somebody?*

It's hard to let another person know what you've been hiding, because it's something you don't want another person to know about. That's why you've been hiding it.

I pictured myself reading my deep, dark secrets to my sponsor, and I let myself feel what I was feeling. I was ashamed of what I'd written. *Fear* and *pride*. They reminded me of an old pair of fuzzy slippers I owned that had holes in the soles and probably fleas in the fur. Repulsive as they were, they were so-o-o-o comfortable. I didn't want to let go of *them*, either.

Once I saw why I was unwilling, I became willing. I didn't have to keep wearing the old slippers. I was beginning to feel better in the new ones.

There are valid reasons for reading your inventory to someone else—someone you trust, as I trust my sponsor. You can read it to a priest, a minister, a rabbi, a good friend who is willing to listen and not judge, a doctor, a therapist—anyone in whom you have confidence. It may be difficult to read it to a family member, because he or she is frequently *in* it.

Q. *Why read it at all?*

For a number of reasons:

1. It forces you to be honest with yourself. At least it did me.

When I was a newcomer and my sponsor sent me home to write something, I wanted to impress her with my writing. I read what I had written: "I am a plant that started as a perfect seed, but grew crookedly and became entangled with other plants—" and so on. I thought it was terrific when I wrote it, but as a I read it—waxing more and more poetic—I knew I was full of it. I had written it to impress my sponsor, and reading it out loud let me see that. I started to laugh, and then so did she.

"You're going to tell me to keep it simple, right?"

"I don't have to."

2. If you don't read it to someone, it enables you to keep your secret demons to yourself. And the whole point is to let go of them.

3. You discover that your feelings and defects are not unique. You're no better and no worse than anyone else. That's ego-smashing, which feels good once you are willing to accept it; it's also confidence-building, which feels good once you are able to accept it.

4. You don't have to be two people anymore. The person on the outside is the same as the person on the inside, because there's nothing to hide. Well, a lot *less* to hide, anyway. It's a freeing experience.

12

A Trip to the Ocean
Letting Go of Blame

Once I had finished my inventory, I had a most curious reaction. I was willing and able to see the part I had played in all the incidents I had written about. I saw what I had done to myself, but what about what the others had done to *me*? I mean, sure, it was my reactions to what my husband had done to me that caused my unhappiness, but that didn't negate what *he* had done to me that made me react that way in the first place. After all, if he hadn't gotten drunk, I wouldn't have gotten mad! It was still his fault, no matter how many inventories I took. It was still *all* their faults. I told that to my sponsor in no uncertain terms.

SPONSOR: So what feeling are you filled with?
ME: Blame!
SPONSOR: Do you like being filled with that?
ME: No, but there's nothing I can do about what *they* did to *me*.
SPONSOR: Sure there is.
ME: Have you forgotten what you've told me over and over? I can't make anyone change but myself. I'm powerless over them, remember?

I had her this time.

SPONSOR: I wasn't thinking of trying to make somebody else change. Your blame isn't hurting somebody else. It's hurting you.
ME: I can't deny my feeling!
SPONSOR: No. But once you know what it is, you can be willing to let go of it.

ME: But what they did to me is *their* problem. Let them suffer for it. They can do their own damn inventory!

SPONSOR: Can you make them?

ME: No, but I'd like to.

SPONSOR: Are you willing to let go of power you don't have?

ME: My God, we're back to square one again.

SPONSOR: No, we're not. We're just having a little slip.

ME: Maybe I just can't face another tool right now.

SPONSOR: Okay. Call me when you're ready. Are you still doing your "gratefuls" and "did wells"?

ME: No. I'm sick of writing.

SPONSOR: I know how you feel. I've felt that way more than once. But "gratefuls" and "did wells" helped me get through seeing all those defects I was filled with when I did my inventory work. You really are recovering, you know.

ME: I don't feel like it right now. I feel like a victim. When I get off my pity pot, I'll give you a call.

SPONSOR: I understand.

For the next few weeks I went around feeling sorry for myself. When I got sick and tired of my self-pity, I called my sponsor and we got together. I was very glad to see her.

ME: Okay, let's get to work. What's next?

SPONSOR: Next comes half the fun.

I stared at her.

SPONSOR: Are you willing to go through the defects in your inventory one more time?

ME: What's the fun in that?

SPONSOR: You get to forgive others for what you think they did to you, and you get to forgive yourself for all your defects.

ME: How?

SPONSOR: Go to a spot where you won't be disturbed. Let yourself *feel* each one of the feelings in each defect.

ME: Why?

SPONSOR: Because once you've experienced each feeling, you can let it go.

ME: But how?

SPONSOR: I can tell you how *I* did it. I asked my higher power to help me.

ME: You know I'm not comfortable with that.

SPONSOR: Okay. Do it by yourself.

ME: I don't know how.

SPONSOR: Are you willing to act *as if* you believed there is a higher power?

ME: I'm willing to believe that the ocean is a power greater than I am.

SPONSOR: Then go to the ocean, and take your defects with you.

ME: Every one of them on the list?

SPONSOR: Every one of them. Close your eyes, and feel them drifting off to sea, one at a time.

ME: That's going to take forever.

SPONSOR: Not as long as it took to acquire them.

I had no "Yes, but—" for that one.

It didn't take nearly as long as I thought it would. When it was over, I noticed that my shoulders were farther from my neck, my breathing was even, my mind was at peace, and I was crying very softly. I went home, had a long soak in the tub, hugged my family, and went to bed.

I never know what serenity is going to feel like until I've felt it.

I noticed in working the tools that I found myself crying many times. Don't be concerned if that happens to you. Change is hard. Habits run deep. Wills are stubborn. Growth is slow. Progress is difficult. Letting go of an old feeling—like blame, for example—may cause you to go through a period of mourning. It's not uncommon for us to mourn the loss of something that belonged to us for so long, even a painful feeling.

QUESTION

Q. *It all sounds too easy to me. Just because you let go of your defects one day doesn't mean they won't come back the next. Do you expect me to believe that blame goes away just like that?*

No, I don't. I expect that I'll always have *some* old blame for somebody, and new blame will crop up, and self-blame will still be one of my biggest problems. The difference is that I'm less afraid to call it what it is now, it's occurring less, and it's much less permanently cemented somewhere inside me.

Why? Because I can name it, claim it, and forgive whoever it is I'm blaming by being willing to let go of whatever it is I'm blaming them for.

More often than not, the recipient of the blame is me. I have to forgive myself for something almost every day. I sometimes look in the mirror and make myself say the words, "I forgive you." I sometimes crawl into bed and say the words there, over and over, until I can actually feel the blame go away.

The next tool was also an enormous help to me in dealing with my defects.

13

One Step Closer
Letting Go of Self-Righteousness

I was powerless, I was making choices, I was detaching with love, I was finished with my inventory, and I had forgiven everybody.

ME: (*laid back*) I'm so serene. I'm beginning to be a "bliss ninny."

SPONSOR: Great.

ME: I mean, I feel really good about myself.

SPONSOR: You should. You've worked hard, and it's paid off.

ME: That's right.

SPONSOR: So would you like to stop here?

ME: You mean there's more?

SPONSOR: It's a process. You don't get a diploma.

ME: *Yes, but—*

Did I see a flicker of humor in her eye?

ME: The way I feel right now, I can handle anything.

SPONSOR: Wonderful. Then you're ready for the next tool. Do you have the list of others you named in the inventory?

ME: The ones I forgave?

SPONSOR: Uh-huh.

ME: Sure. Why?

SPONSOR: Because it's time to look at the harm you did them.

I sat up.

ME: The harm *I* did *them*? Is this some kind of a joke, or what?

SPONSOR: Okay. Maybe you're not ready yet.

ME: Ready for what?

SPONSOR: Making amends to others.

I stood up.

ME: For what *they* did to me?

SPONSOR: No. For what *you* did to them.

ME: Listen, *my husband was the drunk! He's the one who caused all our scenes!*

SPONSOR: Does knowing that make you feel better?

ME: *No, but—*

SPONSOR: Do you want even more peace of mind, with others as well as yourself?

ME: *Yes, but—* (*I've got to stop this!*) Yes, I do, damn it!

SPONSOR: That's why you make amends.

ME: Listen, the person I harmed more than anybody else was myself.

SPONSOR: Then you'll owe yourself more amends than anybody else.

ME: I can understand making amends to myself, but I can't understand making amends to others. *They* have to make the amends. Then we'll *all* find peace of mind.

SPONSOR: Okay. Go and make them make amends.

Powerless again! Will I never learn? I sat down.

SPONSOR: You forgave your husband for *his* behavior. You make amends to him for yours. That's the part you played in the incident.

ME: But I wouldn't have behaved like *I* did if he hadn't behaved like *he* did.

SPONSOR: Then what you're telling me is that your behavior depends upon someone else's.

I didn't like seeing that one at all.

SPONSOR: That makes that someone else a power greater than you. Do you want to give another person that kind of power for the rest of your life?

ME: I don't *want* to make amends.

SPONSOR: I didn't either.

ME: Why *did* you?

SPONSOR: My sponsor told me that my will was standing in the way of my serenity. Just like yours is.

ME: So what am I supposed to do about it?

SPONSOR: I can tell you what *I* did about it. I surrendered my will.

ME: I have no idea what you're talking about.

SPONSOR: Is the ocean still your power greater than yourself?

ME: Sure.

SPONSOR: Let's say that you decide to take a walk along the beach, and when you get there, the tide's in.

ME: That's happened to me.

SPONSOR: Good. Now, let's say that you really *want* to take that walk at that moment, and not get wet.

ME: I wouldn't be able to.

SPONSOR: Right. But you still *wanted* to. Could you *will* the tide to go out?

ME: No.

SPONSOR: So, you could be filled with anger or frustration or disappointment if you kept pursuing your will, right?

ME: Right.

SPONSOR: What would make your life easier?

ME: Waiting until low tide to take my walk.

SPONSOR: Is that following your will?

ME: No. It's following the ocean's.

SPONSOR: And what's the ocean to you?

ME: A power greater than myself.

SPONSOR: And following the will of a power greater than yourself brings you more contentment than still wanting what you can't have.

ME: True.

SPONSOR: Well, I *wanted* serenity, but I had to make amends first. I didn't *want* to make amends. I had to surrender my will to find serenity.

ME: Yes, but—I still don't *want* to make amends.

SPONSOR: Call me if you change your mind.

It took me six months. And by that time I wanted some serenity so badly, I made the call.

At this point, I know that I'm losing some readers. Resistance is a natural reaction to what looms as a humiliating experience. It won't *be* a humiliating experience, by the way. It will be a freeing one. But, if you're like me, you will be full of fear. Don't give up. You're learning these tools for you. Look how far you've come already. You got through that; you can get through this. Be willing to let go of it. We're all so used to drama, we forget that comedy is also an option. Don't make it such a big deal.

14

If You've Named It and Claimed It, You Can Dump It
Letting Go of Pride

Although I had agreed in my last meeting with my sponsor that I would be willing to begin to learn how to use the amends tool, my resistance had returned by the time I saw her again.

I didn't care if this new tool could release me from the past. I didn't care that it was a way to start a new growth process that could last a lifetime. I didn't care that by making amends I could feel the immediate benefits. The thought of making amends was humiliating, and *that* was what I cared about.

Why did I seem to get the words *humility* and *humiliation* confused?

humility/n./ the condition of being humble
humiliation/n./ a lowering of self-respect

The dictionary didn't seem to get the words confused.

SPONSOR: Are you ready for the other half of the fun?
ME: Embarrassment is not fun.
SPONSOR: What feeling *is* embarrassment?
ME: Pride.
SPONSOR: Do you like that feeling?
ME: No, b—
SPONSOR: Are you willing to let go of it?
ME: Yes, b—
SPONSOR: Then go ahead.

She wouldn't let me play my game anymore.

SPONSOR: Get out your list of defects on the black raspberry ice-cream incident.

ME: Oh, not that dumb thing again.

SPONSOR: (*as calm as ever*) It's always a good one to start with.

She had me write the heading "Amends" next to the list of defects. Then we figured out to whom or what I owed amends.

"Childhood theft" is a good situation to start out with because it's so easy to see. It's material. By starting out with something you can actually see, it becomes easier to deal with abstract types of situations, those that deal only with feelings.

Defects	Amends to:	
	Others	Self
1. *Dishonesty (theft)*	Devito's ice-cream store	
2. *Greed*	Mrs. Eckles and store	
3. *Blame*	Mrs. Eckles	
4. *Pride*	Mrs. Eckles	
5. *Self-justification*	Mrs. Eckles	
6. *Anger/Resentment*	Mrs. Eckles	
7. *Judgment*	Mrs. Eckles	
8. *Revenge*	Mrs. Eckles	
9. *Fear*		Me
10. *Guilt*		Me
11. *Lack of self-esteem*		Me
12. *Self-pity*	Mrs. Eckles	
13. *Self-righteousness*	Mrs. Eckles	

You make the amends to the person you harmed because of the defect. I discovered that fear was at the core of all my defects. It ruled me. I stole because I was afraid to ask for something I wanted. I judged because I was afraid of being judged. I resented because I was afraid of the other. I lied because I was afraid to tell the truth. I felt guilty and lacked self-esteem because I was afraid I was bad. And on and on.

Fear, guilt, and lack of self-esteem were "the big three" self-amends. All the rest I owed to others.

ME: Okay. Now what?
SPONSOR: Now, when you're willing, you can make the amends.
ME: Mrs. Eckles is dead! It's too late.

Pause.

ME: What do I do?
SPONSOR: You can write to Mrs. Eckles.
ME: That makes no sense at all!
SPONSOR: Are you doing the amends to make Mrs. Eckles feel better?
ME: I'm doing them to make *me* feel better!
SPONSOR: Write the letter, and see how you feel.

I wrote it and read it to her.

ME: "Dear Mrs. Eckles: I stole black raspberry ice cream from your store, and I lied about it, because you would have been mad if I had told you the truth. I'm not really a thief, but you never gave me any ice cream, so I had to steal it."
SPONSOR: Feel better?
ME: No.
SPONSOR: How come?
ME: I—I'm still justifying it.
SPONSOR: Want to try it again?
ME: "Dear Mrs. Eckles: I stole black raspberry ice cream from your store, and I lied to you about it. I was greedy, and I justified my greed. I was ashamed, so I lied to you about being okay. I judged you, too, and I was wrong. I'm sorry I did that."

This one did feel better. She suggested I let go of it now. I tore it up and threw it into the ocean. I think Mrs. Eckles got it, because I got a "message" back from her. She forgave me.

ME: Okay. Am I finished with this one?

SPONSOR: Is your list of amends taken care of?

ME: There's nothing I can do about what I already stole.

SPONSOR: Sure, there are lots of things you can do.

ME: (*fearing the worst—*) What? (*—and it came*)

SPONSOR: Well, you can go to an ice-cream store. And you can buy one of the customers some ice cream.

ME: They'll think I'm nuts!

SPONSOR: What's that feeling?

ME: Embarrassment!

SPONSOR: What's the defect?

ME: Pride.

SPONSOR: Are you willing to let go of that defect?

ME: I already did!

SPONSOR: Defects come back. Are you willing to let go of pride again?

ME: Yes, but—no, but—. Oh, I give up.

And I went to an ice-cream store. Not right away. I wasn't *that* willing.

I walked into the store and bought myself an ice-cream cone. There were no other customers. Saved! Well, at least I'd tried.

A young woman came in. Oh, God. I stood there. She walked up to the counter and looked at the flavors.

It was now or never. If I put it off, it would only get tougher. What was I afraid of? I had to get on with it.

"Excuse me," I said. "I know this will seem a little crazy, but . . . when I was very young, I stole some ice cream and I want to make amends for the theft. And so—can I buy you whatever it is you were going to buy for yourself?" (Oh, please, don't let her laugh.)

She began to smile. I braced myself.

"I'd love it."

I was stunned. "You would?"

"I think that's great! I have a few amends I have to make myself, I can tell you that."

"You do? Have two scoops."

It was amazing. I was feeling better and lighter. I didn't know why, but it was working.

QUESTIONS

Q. *But making amends for stealing ice cream is certainly not the same as making amends for something really serious. How does one help you with the other?*

No, it isn't the same. Something like stealing ice cream is easier to let go of because you can get a better perspective of it. You *know* intellectually that no matter how big it felt at the time, it was not that big.

But as I was learning how to take my own inventory and make my own amends, I was also discovering that the defects standing in the way of the amends for theft were exactly the same defects standing in the way of the amends for the physical fight with my husband. Pride, fear, resentment, guilt, self-pity—the old standbys. There aren't that many defects in toto. They just keep reappearing again and again.

In fact, let's do an amends for a really serious incident. You've read the fight scene involving my husband and me in the car on page 97 and seen the list of defects I wrote for it on page 98. Let's see what amends I could make, and to whom.

Defects	*Amends to:*	
	Others	Self
1. *Rage*	Husband	
2. *Pride*	Husband	
3. *Fear*		Me
4. *Resentment*	Husband	
5. *Self-pity*	Husband	
6. *Self-justification*	Husband	
7. *Guilt*		Me
8. *Lack of self-esteem*		Me
9. *Self-righteousness*	Husband	

Clearly, I owed my husband amends for my part in the incident. Here's what I wrote, and read to my sponsor:

> The night we had the fight in the car, I was full of rage and wanted to hurt you. I wanted to take revenge. I was self-righteous and self-pitying. I am very sorry I acted the way I did.

I felt comfortable reading it, so I put the paper down and made an amends to my husband. When I was finished, I hugged him, and he hugged me back. But, once again, that's not why I make amends. I can't look for what he'll do or won't do. If I look for the response I think he should make, or one I think he will make, I become a sitting duck for my own expectations. And expectations are duck killers.

The one sure thing in all the amends I've made is that the responses were full of surprises.

What if I have made sure that I didn't push any old buttons, or justified my actions, or tried to prove my "rightness," and still the one I've made up to remains angry or hurt or wants to "get back into it"?

I can't control the outcome. Whatever the reaction of the "amendee," I can let go of the part I played in the incident I'm making amends for. I can refuse to get back into it. I can forgive both of us. I am powerless over the rest.

> **Q.** *I still don't get it. Your husband hit you first. He was wrong. Why did you make amends to him?*
>
> I'm not trying to make me wrong and him right. It is no longer a question of right and wrong. The part he played is something for him to deal with, or not. The part I played is something for *me* to deal with, or not. I'm choosing to make amends so that I can feel better about my life. This point so quickly disappears when pride appears. I know I needed a constant reminder, particularly in the beginning, when I hadn't yet had much experience in feeling better as a result of making amends. As I got used to that feeling, I was more willing to make amends.

Q. *I understand making amends to a recovering addict. But why should I make amends to a practicing addict?*

Remember why you make amends. You make amends for *you*, because doing so brings you some peace of mind. Our minds can do flip-flops because of our old belief systems.

EXERCISE

I think it's time for you to try an amends. Recall the exercise you did in your notebook in which you acted as though you were the son whose father is an addict, and you listed your feelings and defects. Please review your list of defects.

The father is still using. He is still dunning the son for money to support his habit. The son gives the father money but resents doing it. The son decides to make an amends to the father.

Before we look at the amends the son made, I'd like you to write an amends to the father, as though he were *your* father and you his son. Check it over to make sure that the amends itself won't require another amends; that is, try not to open an old wound by putting your dad on the defensive. Make no accusations. Avoid starting out like this: "Look, because you're a junkie, you're driving me crazy. I'm sorry."

Okay—try one. In your notebook, label it "A Son's Amends." After you've written yours, read what the son wrote.

A SON'S AMENDS

The last time you asked me for money, I became very angry with you. I was full of self-righteousness, judgment, and resentment. I'm sorry. My will is the problem. I try to control you. I have no right to do that. I love you. I will always love you. If I can do anything to help you, I'm here for you. But money is not the answer for me. I am uncomfortable doing that. The only thing I can do is let you know that I care.

Do you see any similarities between your amends and the son's? Are you beginning to get the hang of it?

The son felt better. It was a successful amends for him, and he is gradually becoming more and more willing to let go of his father, with love. His obsession is diminishing, even though his father continues to use.

Today, there is a difference in their relationship. They speak on the phone, and the son is no longer "at" his father. They occasionally have dinner, and they sometimes have a good time. The father has gone so far as to ask the son for the phone number of a recovery program that the son had suggested earlier. Whether or not the father will make the call—who knows?

But getting him well is not why the son made the amends.

QUESTIONS

Q. *I've made a few amends, but I don't want to make any more for a while. Must I do them all at once?*

I still have several more to go, and I did my inventory two years ago. Take as much time as you like, and choose the manner in which you make them. You can tell the person face-to-face, you can write a letter, or you can make a phone call. Or, you can simply treat the person to whom you owe the amends differently. For example, if you were cruel to someone, you might choose to be kind when you see her next, instead of bringing up an old wound that might be better left alone. There is no one way.

Trust yourself, but don't fool yourself. Be honest about why you're not making an amends. Examine your motive. If it's because you'll be too embarrassed, acknowledge that to yourself, and then make the amends at some point. If it's because you'll hurt someone, avoid that amends. That won't bring you peace of mind. Letting go of your pride will.

You may even choose not to use the tool. Or you may not feel you're ready to use it right now. You may make one or two amends and then wait a bit.

You're in charge of your own life.

Q. *I've tried some inventories and amends. I feel better about the other person, but I'm beginning to dislike myself even more for what I did to them. What can I do?*

You're looking at your own defects and learning to let yourself feel humble. These were not actions I was used to choosing, so I had to get used to letting myself accept them. Today, I can even enjoy them, but I couldn't in the beginning. At first, I had the same experience you're having.

Keep up your "gratefuls" and "did wells." They're a good balance. Also, take a look at the changes that have taken place in you. Do you see any ways in which you've been improving and recovering since the beginning?

Why not make a brief list of changes on a daily basis? If you don't know where to begin, ask yourself some questions. For example:

Has my sense of humor begun to improve?

Are my eyes less on the addict?

Do I feel better?

Do I look better?

Am I taking better care of me?

Did I have any fun today?

Did I share an experience with somebody today?

Did I forgive myself today?

Write "Changes" at the top of your page. And date each addition. Little changes, big changes, it doesn't matter. Just think of something you've done or something you're doing that brings you a little peace where before there was none.

Then, on a bad day, when you feel hopeless, look at your lists of changes and see the hope.

The next tool will also help you to let go of the self-loathing you're currently going through.

REVIEW

Before we move on, let's review what's in your tool kit so far.

1. The concept of *powerlessness* over the alcoholic/addict (and everyone else except yourself).
2. If you are willing to accept powerlessness over others, you will discover that you have the power to make *choices* for yourself.
3. In order to see what your choices are, you have to stand back. You have to *detach with love.*
4. By taking a look at yourself, you become aware that your *reactions* get you into trouble. You can change your reactions.
5. You have to see what your reactions were, because only then can you begin to change what you want to change. To do this, you take your own *inventory* and read it to someone you trust.
6. You *forgive* those who caused you real or imagined harm.
7. You make *amends* to those whom you feel you have harmed.

15

You Owe It to Yourself
Letting Go of "The Big Three"

As you make amends to those you have harmed, don't forget yourself.

Looking over my list of defects, I noticed there wasn't as much variety in the amends I owed to myself. Three basic feelings cropped up over and over again: fear, guilt, and lack of self-esteem. It seemed as though those were the most common weapons I used against myself. And they were more deadly than they at first seemed, since they had been the causes of many of the other defects for which I was making amends to others.

Fear, the biggest of the big three, led me to feelings of *resentment*. How? When my husband was in the throes of his disease, I feared how he would behave with me or with somebody else, and I resented him terribly for that. Fear led me to feelings of *jealousy*. I was afraid when my husband was at a party that he would find someone else and leave me. I was jealous of every woman he talked to.

Lack of self-esteem fed jealousy, too. Feeling the way I did, I was jealous of an attractive woman at the office. Lack of self-esteem made me afraid to speak up at a business meeting, so I sat there feeling sorry for myself. Guilt led me to feelings of *blame* and *anger*, because I felt I had to fix my husband and he wouldn't let me.

I could go on and on with patterns that had become firmly established in my head. And firmly established patterns are not easy to break. You have to see them first.

Do you have any patterns? If you see any, write them down. That's one way to begin breaking them.

I had let "the big three" run my life long enough. I was ready to make amends to myself and run my own life.

But other than forgiving myself my defects—which I had done and was continuing to do on a daily basis—I had no idea of how to go about making amends to myself. I was not used to being good or kind or loving with myself.

I told my sponsor that I was ready but could think of no way to use this tool.

SPONSOR: What does making amends to others make you feel?
ME: As though I'd done something good.
SPONSOR: For whom?
ME: For me.
SPONSOR: And what does that make you feel?
ME: I guess I like myself a little better for having done it.
SPONSOR: And what's that?
ME: Self-esteem.

As I thought about what I was saying, I began to get clearer on what amends to others really was for me.

The more amends I make to others, the less afraid I am to make them. And the act of making them removes some of the guilt I had for having the defects in the first place. So making amends to others is a way to make amends to yourself.

SPONSOR: Exactly. There are others.
ME: I'm ready.
SPONSOR: Pick a fear from your inventory.
ME: I'm afraid to drive on freeways.
SPONSOR: What can take that fear away?
ME: I don't know—what?
SPONSOR: Having the courage to drive on freeways.
ME: *Yes, but—I can't.*
SPONSOR: *Yes, but—you won't.*
ME: You told me not to deny my feelings.
SPONSOR: I never told you not to *let go* of them, once you've accepted them. You're hanging on to your fear. Why not let go of it?

ME: I don't think it'll work.

SPONSOR: What are you afraid of, anyway?

ME: Dying!

SPONSOR: Do you have any control over that?

ME: No.

SPONSOR: What does that make you?

ME: Powerless.

SPONSOR: Are you willing to accept your powerlessness?

ME: Yes, but—

SPONSOR: Go. Drive.

ME: Can I try it at 6:00 A.M. on a Sunday?

SPONSOR: It's your choice.

ME: Can I get off at the first exit?

SPONSOR: It's your choice.

I did it, I'm still doing it, and I'm still here.

Every time I am willing to let go of fear, guilt, or lack of self-esteem, I can make amends to myself by replacing them with courage, self-acceptance, and self-love. Not a bad trade, is it?

I must confess, however, that it's not as easy as it sounds. On some days I'm filled with one, or two, or even all three of "the big three." I don't think they'll ever completely go away. But I can feel them controlling me less and less when I am able to give them a name, take responsibility for them, and then forgive myself for having them.

Most of us are far too hard on ourselves. I try to remind myself every day to do something that I enjoy, to treat myself to something, to look for something I like about myself. Once again, the good old "gratefuls" and "did wells" come in handy.

Be willing to see your fear or your guilt or your lack of self-esteem on a daily basis. Try to recognize it. It belongs to you. After you've named it and claimed it, *dump* it. Try not to hang on to it and let it ruin the rest of your day. Let go of it and substitute an opposite.

Be courageous today.

Accept yourself today.

Love yourself today.

And please remember when you pass a mirror to stop and forgive the person looking back at you.

These are all self-amends, as are your "gratefuls" and "did wells" and your list of changes.

QUESTION

Q. *My granddaughter lives with me. We used to be wonderful pals, but since she got hooked on drugs and alcohol, all she does is criticize me. I have no self-esteem at all. Can you help me?*

I'm so sorry. I know you must be wondering who this stranger is who's living with you.

All I can do is remind you that your granddaughter has a disease, and her cruelty toward you is a result of her disease. There is no question in my mind that she, too, is suffering when she treats you the way she now does. But you and I are both powerless over your granddaughter's disease. I urge you to get help in a support group. Try Nar-Anon or Al-Anon. Try counseling or therapy.

And please don't give up on the tools you have learned. If you are willing to keep working with them, they will work for you.

The next time your granddaughter criticizes you, try detaching with love and looking at her illness instead of listening to her words. If you're comfortable with praying, pray silently for her when she's being mean to you. Let her know she hurts you when she talks that way and suggest that she get help. Give one of your friends a call and share your feelings.

16

A Daily Checkup
Letting Go One Day at a Time

Every time I make an amends to somebody, I remove that part of the inventory from my notebook and burn it. I had great reluctance to do that at first. It was like losing a part of me, and that was, indeed, what I was doing. But I wasn't thrilled with those parts of me anymore, and once I got into the swing of it, it was a very freeing experience.

But the defects I was getting rid of revisited me.

ME: I thought that once I got rid of resentment it would be gone forever, but it comes back.

SPONSOR: Of course it does. All of them do at one time or another. Do you expect yourself to be perfect?

ME: After all that work, I expect to be at least a little *closer* to perfect.

SPONSOR: After all that work, you *are*.

ME: But I don't want those defects to build up again. Not ever.

SPONSOR: All you've done so far is clean up your past.

ME: What's left? My future?

SPONSOR: How about your present? If you're willing to wipe your blackboard clean today, you won't have to have such a bulging list of inventories and amends ever again. Want a tool to help you?

ME: *(No "Yes, But/No, But" game here. I really wanted this tool!)* Yes!

She suggested that I review my day before going to sleep each night. If I found an incident that was left hanging, I was to do a brief inventory on it.

That night, I found an incident. Not a major one. Not one having to do with the recovering addict in my life.

I find that as I take my eyes off him more and more, I am using the tools less and less on incidents having to do with him. The nice thing is that the tools work in my dealings with everybody. My life isn't changing only in terms of my relationship to my husband. It's changing in relation to everybody else, too. At first, I thought that all those around me were changing. Now I know that it's *my* attitudes, my points of view, my behavioral patterns, and my reactions that are going through a metamorphosis. Of course, others may indeed be changing, too. I don't know about them. But I *do* know about me.

The Incident

My daughter is leaving for a job interview. I look at her and ask, "Are you sure you want to wear *that*?"

She goes into battle stance. "What's wrong with this?"

"Nothing. Never mind. Good luck."

She storms out and slams the door.

I yell after her, "I was only trying to be helpful!"

The moment that scene happened, I could have dumped my self-righteousness, judgment, self-pity, and guilt and run after her, hugged her, told her that I was full of it, that what she wore was none of my business, that she knew better than I did what kids wear to interviews today, that I was sorry, and that I hoped she'd knock 'em dead!

I could have, but that well I'm not. Oh, every once in a while I am, but it's rare.

Since I didn't run after her, that night after doing my "gratefuls" and "did wells" I reviewed the day, checked for any incidents, picked out my own defects, resolved to make amends the next day, forgave myself, and went to sleep.

The following day I made amends to my daughter (who, by the way, got the job), and I used the amends as a "did well" that night. See how it works?

The more willing I am to let go of my pride in making an

amends, the easier it becomes. And I find it amazing how much closer my relationships are with my family and friends. There's a lot more laughter, too. They don't seem to mind the fact that I'm imperfect. And I don't seem to mind the fact that they are, either.

Trying to hide my imperfections was one of the things that got me into trouble. When I admit my defects on a daily basis, they're no longer secret, and they're no longer demons.

Of course, with daily inventories, there's much less drama in my life, and sometimes I miss it. But not enough to go back onto the stage.

QUESTIONS

Q. *Like your husband, my friend is recovering. I'm learning to use the tools you've suggested, and they're helping me a lot. The daily inventory keeps me out of big trouble, and I feel much more relaxed. But sometimes I think I'm just fooling myself to think I'm getting better. I'm very afraid to be tested. What would happen to me if he started to use again?*

You can't prevent another's slip. If your friend's disease flares up again, your friend has his own tools to help himself.

The tools you have in your tool kit are designed to work whether the chemical dependent is practicing or recovering. Why? Because they're tools for you. Just because your friend has a slip doesn't mean *you* have to.

Instead of worrying about the future, which you know is pointless, why not enjoy today? Your life is working, and you're both in recovery.

By the way, whatever fear you have about your friend, be willing to let go of it, and make some kind of amends to yourself. Make amends to your friend, too, for your lack of trust in him. But avoid telling him you don't trust him. Amends that hurt somebody are not amends. Instead, do something that shows him how much you do trust him. Bake a cake for his next drug-free birthday. Let him borrow something of yours. Show some sign of faith in him.

Q. *I've been working hard on learning to use the tools, and they are helping me to take my eyes off my addicted son. But I find that I'm filled with more and more rage for what is happening to him. I don't even know who the rage is aimed at. But the more I am filled with it, the more I notice myself going around smiling at everybody, even strangers, because I don't want anyone to see the volcano underneath—*

(Can you see that this woman is recovering? She is looking at *herself*!)

—I feel like two different people. I don't like either one of them. Can you help me? I do daily inventories on my feelings, but I'm lost. Who do I owe amends to?

You sound so much like I used to. The more rage I felt underneath toward my husband, the more bubbly I became on the surface to hide the rage.

The dilemma is caused by a form of "people-pleasing." Pleasing people we love makes us feel good. "People-pleasing" does not, because it comes from fear, fear of what people will think of us: "I'm going to please you so that you'll think I'm great, because I don't think I am, and if you saw what was underneath, you wouldn't think so either."

The person you hurt most by people-pleasing is yourself; the amends for people-pleasing are to you.

How do you dump people-pleasing? First, by forgiving yourself for doing it. Second, by being willing to let it go, a little at a time. And third, by being willing to risk not pleasing someone who has just violated your rights.

At the same time you're making self-amends on a daily basis, you may find that the rage that has been covered up by people-pleasing is beginning to surface. Write about how this feels to you, share it with somebody you trust, get help in a support group, get professional help, scream in your car, and forgive yourself if you swing too far on the pendulum when you stop people-pleasing. You may even become something of a holy terror for a while. Sometimes it's the only way to stop being a doormat. Don't worry about it. You'll swing back to the middle eventually.

It's a game. Let go of your fear of being wrong or your need to be right. It works either way, if you're willing to play it.

17

The "Maybe, But—" Game

Letting Go of Having to Know

I had come a long way with my sponsor. After having accepted that addiction is a disease and that I also have my own disease, and having accepted powerlessness, making choices, detachment with love, responsibility for my own reactions, a power greater than I, self-inventory, amends to others, and amends to myself, I was ready to close up and *lock* my tool kit. Enough, already! In fact, I was in an unusual hurry to thank my sponsor and get out. What was going on? What was I avoiding?

ME: Thanks so much for all you've done.

SPONSOR: Are you finished?

ME: No, of course not. I still intend to go to meetings, and I'll call you and check in every once in a while.

SPONSOR: Have you worked on everything with me that you want to work on?

ME: Sure have.

SPONSOR: Well, thanks for giving *me* so much.

ME: Giving *you* so much?

SPONSOR: Sponsoring somebody teaches me a lot.

ME: I'm glad. Thanks for everything.

SPONSOR: You're welcome.

We hugged. She turned her porch light on, and I started out the door.

SPONSOR: How's your praying coming along?

That's *why I wanted to get out.*

ME: Better than my meditating. See you soon.

SPONSOR: How come?

ME: How come what? How come my praying's coming along better? Or my meditating's coming along worse?

SPONSOR: How often do you try either one?

ME: I don't know. Every couple of months, I guess.

SPONSOR: You know, prayer and meditation are helpful tools.

ME: *Maybe, but—*

SPONSOR: Are you willing to try them?

ME: *Maybe, but—*

SPONSOR: Would you like some help?

ME: *Maybe—but—*

No more "Yes, but/no, but." I had at last found a new game, and we both broke up.

I've spent the last couple of years working on both prayer and meditation. I'm better at the former than I am at the latter. I was told that praying is *talking* to God as I understand him and that meditation is *listening* to God as I understand him. That explains why I'm better at praying.

The problem I have is that I don't understand him. I don't understand him at all. But I'm getting more and more willing to talk, if he's willing to listen, and more and more willing to listen, if he's willing to talk. I don't know if he is or isn't willing to listen or talk, but I'm willing to act as if he is.

Why do I keep trying, if I don't believe in God?

For one thing, my sponsor accepts and uses all the tools. And if I want what she has, maybe I have to do the same. But talk about *resistance*!

ME: Do I have to use the word *God*?

SPONSOR: No. Use whatever you like.

ME: I like *higher power* better.

SPONSOR: That's fine.

ME: What should I pray for?

SPONSOR: Guidance.

ME: But what does that mean?

SPONSOR: Whatever it means to you.

ME: Well, it could mean anything—everything—

SPONSOR: Keep it simple.

ME: But I still don't understand.

SPONSOR: Do you understand what the word *guidance* means?

ME: Yes.

SPONSOR: Then just think of what it means and ask for it. Maybe that's all the understanding you need today.

ME: Then what?

SPONSOR: Then you listen.

ME: I don't understand.

SPONSOR: Do you understand what the word *listen* means?

ME: Yes.

SPONSOR: Then just think of listening.

ME: Why should I go through all this?

SPONSOR: What if it works?

In the last couple of years, *something's* been working. I don't know for sure what it is, but when I pray for guidance, I receive guidance. I don't know if that's because I pray for it, or because it just comes, but I'm not taking any chances. Why mess with success?

The guidance is seldom what I expect. Nor does it come when I expect it to come, nor where I expect it to come from. My higher power has a great sense of humor.

What is my higher power? Anything I think my higher power is. Mine changes constantly.

At times, it's the universe. Other times, it's nature itself. Often it's the program, or the meetings, or the tools, or an inner conscience, or an outer force. Once, it was Beethoven's Ninth. Today, it's the feeling of "oneness" with the universe. Yesterday, it was anybody who knew more about something I knew less about. When I hurt, it can be the telephone, because there's always help at the other end. I use various things at various times, and one does not negate another.

The most astonishing thing I've discovered about a higher power is that it doesn't matter to me whether there *is* one or not. The more I allow myself to believe what I choose to believe, the more I let go of my own resistance, and the more I get out of my own way and allow myself to surrender to the spiritual side of my existence, the better my life works. So I don't care whether I'm right or wrong.

And there are still days when *nothing* works, days when I feel alone and without hope. Everything I've learned seems to go out the window, and I can't think of one tool. I try "acting as if," and nothing happens. I can't seem to find my way out of the tunnel. That frightens me, but not nearly as much as it used to. I know that it's my will that has sent me into the darkness, and when I can let go of it, I will find the light. Not necessarily when I want to, but I will find it. Knowing that the light is not far away makes the darkness not as dark and the length of the tunnel not as long as it used to be. As soon as I can name these feelings and claim them, I am able to dump them. Going to the ocean always helps me. I am restored to sanity once more. But on "those days," I forget that the ocean is there.

When my will blinds me to the infinite choices I can make to get help, I'm in a "slip." Oh, yes, *we* can have slips, too, just like the alcoholic/addict. Ours are emotional slips. But don't worry. A slip is temporary, even though it may not feel temporary when you're *in* one. When it's over, forgive yourself. You're human.

I'm working on my meditation today. I choose something that soothes me, and I try to think about it for five minutes. Five minutes is endless! My mind strays, and I *gently* (that's very important) return to the thought. Maybe I'm getting a little better. I don't know. I'm certainly getting more patient with myself, and that's a "grateful."

I choose to feel a power greater than myself surrounding me when I'm lonely and filling me when I'm afraid. Making that choice, when I am able to remember to make it, leads me to another "grateful." I'll do almost anything that leads to one. Why?

Gratefulness = serenity.

QUESTION

Q. *I simply cannot believe in God. To me it's all hogwash! Does this mean that the tools won't work?*

The only requirement is that you be willing to believe, or to "act as if" you believe, in a power greater than yourself. Otherwise, you'll start playing God, and that *doesn't* work. Acceptance of powerlessness (over others) *is* a necessary tool, at least for me.

The Serenity Prayer helps me to understand the concept of powerlessness:

> God grant me the serenity to accept the things I cannot change (*that's everything and everybody but me*), the courage to change the things I can (*those things that have to do with me; the tools help me to make these changes*), and the wisdom to know the difference.

"The wisdom to know the difference" is the hardest part for me. What can I change? What can't I change? I *always* forget. I have to keep reminding myself that I can change only me. No matter how hard I try, *I am powerless* over everybody and everything else. And, as I write this, I believe it. But tomorrow—?

What It's Like Now

Letting Go with Love

18

Passing Them On

We've come to the final tool, and if you learn to use this one, you'll hit the jackpot every time. I think of it as my reward for working so hard on all the other tools. What is this piece of cake?

If you feel that the tools we've worked on together have been, and will continue to be, of value to you, consider sharing them with someone out there who needs your help. I'm sure there's someone out there who does.

The final tool is being willing to give all the tools away, because that's the only way you can keep them. That's why my sponsor sponsors me, and that's why I sponsor others. The return on the investment is limitless.

ME: So you don't believe there is a power greater than you?
NEWCOMER: I can't!
ME: How about substituting the word *won't*?
NEWCOMER: All right, I won't.
ME: The tools are easier if you're willing to believe in a power greater than yourself.
NEWCOMER: Easier for you, maybe.
ME: Easier for me?
NEWCOMER: You're not as stubborn as I am.

I couldn't help smiling.

ME: You admitted that you never had, do not have, and never will have any power over your father. What does that make you?
NEWCOMER: Powerless.
ME: Are you willing to surrender that power?
NEWCOMER: Yes, but—

Here we go again.

ME: Do you want to hang on to something you don't have?
NEWCOMER: No, but—
ME: Would you like to drive to the ocean with me?

I can't believe it. Me, a former basket case, sponsoring a newcomer. I'm getting better. She's getting better. You're getting better. Even when we have enormous slips, the tools work in spite of us.

19

A Grateful Passenger

We've been on quite a journey together.

I, for one, will be in the same boat for the rest of my life. But today I'm enjoying the trip. The storms still come up, but I'm not afraid I'll fall overboard anymore. The passengers in the boat are my friends. I was such a lonely passenger before. Today, I'm a grateful one.

The changes that have taken place in me, and that are continuing to take place in me, are astonishing. Not only am I healthier than I was while my husband was drinking and after he found sobriety, but I'm also healthier than I was before I met my husband! Now, that's *progress.*

Supermarkets are now a breeze for me.

Freeways are not, but I'm able to drive on them for several miles without the old panic. It gets easier all the time.

I still get depressed, but I don't stay depressed. Knowing that, I don't get *as* depressed.

I still have the old defects, but they don't last as long or go as deep.

I still worry, but much, much less.

I laugh at myself a lot.

My sense of humor grows with me.

I can experience serenity.

I'm willing to take a risk.

I have less guilt for yesterday and less fear of tomorrow.

I keep my mouth shut when it's time to listen. (Not often enough, but a little more.)

I express my discomfort when I feel it, before it turns into rage.

Where do these changes come from? From my being willing to "get off it," "come off it," "surrender it," "release it," "turn it over"—whatever the "it" is that I'm stuck on, worried about, obsessed with, or hanging on to. These changes come from my "letting go with love."

Change = growth.

And I grow a little every day.

When I was a newcomer to the program, I heard someone share that he was grateful for the addict in his life, because without her he would not have found the program. I could not comprehend what he was saying then. Now I can.

I hope—and, yes, I pray—that you have been helped along the way. If I am willing to see myself as a conduit (and I am, when I can get out of my own way), then I can take no credit for what's on these pages. I can take no blame, either. That's the closest I've ever come to spiritual enlightenment. For now, that's close enough.

I've been given a new life. I am humbled by the experience. I owe it all to Al-Anon. Whatever tools I have came from the program. Whatever wisdom I have learned in using these tools also came from the program. However successful I've been in sharing my experience, strength, and hope with you is a direct result of my having had others in the program share their experiences, strengths, and hopes with me. Whatever comfort and support you have found in this book has come from the comfort and support the program has given me.

It's a program of attraction rather than promotion. But if you want what I have, you'll find it there a thousandfold. Written pages can in no way substitute for the experience of just one meeting. And the experience of one meeting can in no way substitute for the experience of many meetings.

QUESTIONS

Q. *I might like to try a meeting. Who do I call?*

Look up Al-Anon in your phone book. It is probably listed as "Al-Anon Family Groups." If you find nothing, call the Al-Anon Family Group Headquarters in New York City. (You'll find phone numbers for all these organizations in the Resources section at the end of this book.) They'll help you. If you can't find a phone number for Nar-Anon or Coc-Anon by calling Al-Anon, you may be able to find the numbers by looking up Narcotics Anonymous or Cocaine Anonymous in your phone book. Families Anonymous may also be available to you. Adult Children of Alcoholics another possibility.

Q. *What's the difference between these programs?*

The principles are the same. Traditionally, Al-Anon is for relatives and friends of alcoholics, Nar-Anon is for the relatives and friends of drug abusers, Cocanon is for the relatives and friends of cocaine addicts, and Families Anonymous is for the relatives and friends of either. A.C.A. is self-explanatory. Today, however, cross-addiction is so common that you, as a relative or friend, may qualify for any or all of these programs.

Q. *Will my joining a program help the addict?*

It often does. But there are no guarantees. Your participation in a program will help you.

Q. *I'm thirteen. My mom is an alcoholic. Can I go to Al-Anon?*

You can, but you might feel more comfortable with Alateen, a special-interest group of the Al-Anon Family Groups, intended for teenagers. Call your local Al-Anon office for the number.

Q. *What is the youngest age at which a child can start in a program?*

Al-Atot, another special-interest group of the Al-Anon Family Groups, is for children up to eight years of age. Then there are the preteen groups for children eight to thirteen.

Q. *How do you join one of these support groups?*

There are no dues, no fees, and nothing to sign. If you go to a meeting, you belong.

Q. *I think my sister is an alcoholic, but I'm not sure. Do I still qualify for Al-Anon?*

It's not up to us to determine someone else's alcoholism. Anyone whose life is affected by someone else's drinking qualifies.

Q. *I'm a recovering alcoholic whose grandson is a practicing alcoholic. Can I go to Al-Anon?*

Yes, as long as you share at Al-Anon meetings from an Al-Anon point of view.

Would you look at these questions? The passengers are all in recovery. They've chosen to let go of trying to handle their problems alone.

In case you're wondering, my husband and I are still together. We work our programs differently but we continue to work our programs, and the respect and compassion we're learning to feel for ourselves we're learning to feel for each other.

Our relationship is not problem-free, but whatever comes up doesn't last as long nor run as deep. We each have our own tools that continue to help us.

Most important of all, we see hope in a relationship that, not long ago, felt hopeless. There is more laughter in our home today than ever before. That's both a "grateful" *and* a "did well."

And now it's time for me to let go, with love. How about one last "Review"? (You didn't think I'd let you get away that easily, did you?)

20

The Ultimate Review

Following are the original Twelve Steps of Alcoholics Anonymous. Al-Anon, and all the other anonymous programs mentioned in this book, as well as the tools we've been dealing with, are based on these Twelve Steps. This is the *ultimate* review, and it never ends. If you choose to stay on board, *bon voyage!*

1. We admitted we were powerless over alcohol (*If the addict is recovering, substitute what you are powerless over today—such as everything and everybody but you. Try "people, places, and events"*)—that our lives had become unmanageable.
2. Came to believe that a Power greater than ourselves could restore us to sanity.
3. Made a decision to turn our will and our lives over to the care of God as we understood him.
4. Made a searching and fearless moral inventory of ourselves.
5. Admitted to God, to ourselves, and to another human being the exact nature of our wrongs.
6. Were entirely ready to have God remove all these defects of character.
7. Humbly asked him to remove our shortcomings.
8. Made a list of all persons we had harmed and became willing to make amends to them all.
9. Made direct amends to such people wherever possible, except when to do so would injure them or others.
10. Continued to take personal inventory, and when we were wrong promptly admitted it.
11. Sought through prayer and meditation to improve our conscious contact with God as we understood him,

praying only for knowledge of his will for us and the power to carry that out.

12. Having had a spiritual awakening as the result of these Steps, we tried to carry this message to others,* and to practice these principles in all our affairs.

Millions upon millions of people are being helped in Twelve Steps programs, which are growing at such an amazing rate that I'm convinced there is one for everyone. Just imagine: people-to-people spiritual therapy around the world. No leaders, no fees, no dues, and no last names, and all we have to give up is the misery that brought us together in the first place. Not a bad deal, come to think of it.

---

*In the original Twelve Steps, this phrase is "we tried to carry the message to other alcoholics." The version quoted here is the Al-Anon version.

The Twelve Steps have been reprinted by permission of Alcoholics Anonymous and Al-Anon Family Group Headquarters, Inc..

Resources

The books and organizations listed below are frequently selected as sources of information for people interested in learning more about problems relating to alcoholism and drug addiction. These sources offer diverse opinions, and their listing here is not to be considered an endorsement of their individual points of view.

BOOKS

Addictive Drinking: The Road to Recovery for Problem Drinkers and Those Who Love Them, by Clark Vaughan. Penguin Books, 40 W. 23rd St., New York, NY 10010.

Adult Children of Alcoholics, by Janet G. Woititz, Ed.D. Health Communications, Inc., 1721 Blount Rd., Suite #1, Pompano Beach, FL 33069; (800) 851-9100.

Al-Anon's Twelve Steps and Twelve Traditions. Al-Anon Family Group Headquarters, Box 182, Madison Square Station, New York, NY 10159-0182.

Another Chance: Hope and Health for Alcoholic Families, by Sharon Wegsheider-Cruse. Science and Behavior Books, Box 60519, Palo Alto, CA 94306.

The Big Book. Alcoholics Anonymous World Services, Box 459, Grand Central Station, New York, NY 10163.

Children of Alcoholism, by Judith Seixas and Geraldine Youcha. Harper and Row, 10 East 53rd St., New York, NY 10022.

Codependent No More, by Melody Beatty. Hazelden Educational Materials, Box 176, Pleasant Valley Road, Center City, MN 55012-0176.

The Courage to Change, by Dennis Wholey. Houghton Mifflin Company, 2 Park Street, Boston, MA 02108.

Loving an Alcoholic: Help and Hope for Significant Others, by Jack Mumey. Contemporary Books, 180 N. Michigan Ave., Chicago, IL 60601.

A Primer on Adult Children of Alcoholics, by Timmen L. Cermak, M.D., Health Communications, Inc., 1721 Blount Rd., Suite #1, Pompano Beach, FL 33069; (800) 851-9100.

The Twelve Steps and Twelve Traditions. Alcoholics Anonymous World Services, Box 459, Grand Central Station, New York, NY 10163.

Women Who Love Too Much, by Robin Norwood. Jeremy P. Tarcher, Inc., 9110 Sunset Blvd., Los Angeles, CA 90069.

CATALOGS

Books, brochures, and audio and video cassettes on all issues related to substance abuse are available through the following:

Al-Anon Family Group Headquarters, Box 182, Madison Square Station, New York, NY 10159-0182; (800) 356-9996.

Alcoholics Anonymous World Services, Box 459, Grand Central Station, New York, NY 10163; (212) 686-1100.

CompCare Publications, 2415 Annapolis Lane, Minneapolis, MN 55441; (800) 328-3330.

Hazelden Educational Materials, Box 176, Pleasant Valley Road, Center City, MN 55012-0176; (800) 328-9000, (Minnesota: (800) 257-0070).

Health Communications, Inc., 1721 Blount Rd., Suite #1, Pompano Beach, FL; (800) 851-9100.

The Johnson Institute, 510 First Avenue N., Minneapolis, MN 55403; (800) 231-5165, (Minnesota: (800) 247-0484).

WHERE TO CALL FOR HELP

Consult your local information directory for the district office nearest you, or call:

Al-Anon/Alateen World Services: (800) 356-9996.

Alcoholics Anonymous World Services: (212) 686-1100.

Cocanon: (213) 859-2206 or (212) 713-5133.

Families Anonymous World Services: (818) 989-7841.

Nar-Anon Family Group Headquarters: (213) 547-5800.

National Association for Children of Alcoholics (A.C.A. Central Service): (213) 464-4423.